M000298608

Tales For The Masses

Stories Connecting Scripture
And Everyday Life

Deacon Tim Healy

CSS Publishing Company, Inc.
Lima, Ohio

Introduction

Fr. John Powers, C.P., is a fabulous Catholic author who likes to tell "true stories that never happened." I chatted with him briefly about this one day, since I like to do the same thing. He winked and said with a grin, "They're actually true stories that really *do* happen, all the time."

I laughed, since I knew what he meant and knew that it was true. A good story simply never betrays whether its origins lie entirely in fact or entirely in fantasy. So I leave it to you whether or not to believe that this conversation with Fr. John actually happened, but even if it didn't, of course, it did!

Stories help everyone connect the message of the gospel with everyday life. My friend, Fr. Ron May, used to tell me to see to it that my homilies told "God's story, the people's story and my own story." Taken together with Fr. Powers' observation, it seems that a good story, literally factual or not, is a pretty good vehicle for composing homilies that resonate with people's lived experience.

The stories in this book come from homilies I've written over the last decade. Some were inspired by stories I'd read or heard, but the innermost insights within them are essentially original. I'd thought about publishing the homilies wholesale, but my daughter Katie suggested that people were more likely to read stories and draw their own conclusions than to read homilies and have the meaning served up. She is far wiser than I will ever be, so that's what I've done, with just a few exceptions. There's a table in the back of the book that associates each story with a reading in the lectionary.

I would like to thank my lovely daughter, Katie, for pointing out the best way to go at getting this material out, Professor Robin Martinelli for insisting that I do so before I die, and my wonderful wife, Chris, who is proof that there is a God, and that God is good. Thanks also to everyone who read this while it was still a work in progress, for their acute insights and encouragement. They are as much evidence as anyone would need of the reality of the communion of the saints!

Enjoy!

Acknowledgments

Murphy The Grump

There's a story about Murphy the Grump and his wife Drusilla that illustrates how God transforms. He and his wife Drusilla had arrived at an uneasy *modus vivendi* of sorts after many years of marriage. He would ignore her except when there was something to complain about, and she would leave him alone unless he annoyed her. Their patience with one another had vanished over time, giving way to a sullen form of mutual neglect. Their grown children and their families could feel the chill and rarely came around.

One day Murphy woke up, looked at his wife asleep next to him and wondered, "Is this all there is?" Once upon a time, he had fallen in love with this person beside him. How had it changed into this? Who could know? It couldn't be fixed, he thought, and probably wasn't worth fixing anyway. He sighed, got up and went off to work, as usual.

No one at work had ever seen Murphy smile. It wasn't that he was mean, it was just that there was nothing joyful about him. As it turned out, a new guy had recently arrived in the office. "One of those Christians," Murphy figured. "Always smiling as if there was something worth being joyful about, the pain in the neck."

Another annoying thing about the Christian was that he was always doing something you didn't expect, to try to cheer you up. Murphy had decided he didn't need this guy, and tried to avoid him.

Murphy went to his cubicle that day, slumped into his seat and realized he'd sat down on something. He got up, turned around, and there was a sign with rainbows, butterflies, and daisies on his chair that said, "Have a great day — God loves you!" It was the Christian again. Murphy took the sign, ripped it up loudly, and threw it in the trash.

Just then the phone rang. Murphy picked it up and noticed that there was a Post-it note across the handset that said "Be joyful — God loves you!" Murphy took it off and put it aside, thinking to himself he knew exactly where he was going to stick *that* Post-it note next.

It was the receptionist on the phone. She told him his flowers were here and to come pick them up. Murphy hadn't ordered any flowers and he told the receptionist there had been a mistake. She said, "No mistake, they're for you." It was the Christian again, Murphy knew as he headed off to get his flowers.

There was a cluster of people around the receptionist, including that pain in the neck Christian. He turned to go down another hallway but they saw him and called out, "Hey Murphy, great flowers," one said. "Get them for your wife for Mothers' Day?" another asked. "Good man," one of the women remarked, "What a kind thing to do!"

He looked into their eyes and saw something he'd never seen before — something that looked like kindness and compassion, but something that was also inviting, waiting for an answer. In that moment, the Spirit grasped Murphy soul and body and shook him the way an animal shakes something it has caught.

Deep within, Murphy saw unconditional redemption being offered to him, and a power much larger and much deeper than anything he'd ever experienced before urged him to take it. Seized by that power, he saw in a flash that he had been a prisoner of something evil for a long time, and it didn't have to stay that way. He reached out and took the offer.

"Oh yeah," he said. "I forgot I'd ordered them. Mothers' Day. Thanks." For the first time ever, Murphy gave a little smile. The Christian handed him his flowers.

When Murphy got home that night he put the flowers on the kitchen table. Eventually his wife emerged from the darkness and silently glided into the kitchen to slice some slabs of cold meatloaf for dinner.

When she saw the flowers her jaw dropped — the last time she'd seen flowers was at their wedding.

"Who are these for?" Drusilla asked.

"They're for you," Murphy said.

"Who are they from?" she demanded.

back to the old ways and simply conform to his upbringing, but it brings him no peace when he does that.

He's coming to learn the truth of the gospel and the implications of the canticle of Zechariah: "Blessed be the Lord, the God of Israel, for he has come to his people and set them free." The Lord, it seems, will have it no other way.

Are You Going To Be Saved?

Have you ever wondered, as the disciples did in the gospel, whether or not you're going to be saved? Jesus never gave them a straight answer, but has it ever seemed to you like it'd be really nice to get a hint?

As I thought about that I was reminded of similar feelings that I'd had many years ago when I was in college, and everyone's grades used to be posted in public. They didn't use anyone's real name, of course — just your Social Security number and your grade.

When the grades went up, we'd cluster around the bulletin board to find out if we'd made it. Of course, if you worked hard, did well on the exams, and contributed in class, that was all you needed by way of hints along the way about how things would turn out, and there was no good reason to expect a poor outcome. But then again, you never really know until you see your grade in black and white, do you?

It was always an emotionally charged moment as some looked and exclaimed "I got an A!" while others smiled weakly or not at all, and others just moved away quickly and quietly. I remember looking around and wondering who'd gotten what and which poor soul owned that one lonely 'F.'

I remember questioning whether the moment of judgment was going to be something like that. I felt uneasy because, like the disciples in today's gospel, it seemed to me there was no sure way of knowing until death whether you'd passed or failed; whether you were saved or not.

I found the possibility of eternal failure terrifying. I worried that maybe everything good I'd ever done just wouldn't be enough; perhaps there was some terrible evil I'd done that I'd forgotten about, but God had not.

I shared those feelings with my theology professor, Fr. Dave, one day after mass. He smiled and laughed, asking, "What kind of God do you believe in, anyway? Do you think you're destined for hell because you ate a meatball on Friday during Lent when you were nine?"

Then he explained that the whole intent of the good news was not to threaten us, but to light a fire under us; to bring our faith out of our heads down into our hearts and out into the world.

"Some folks don't seem to see that faith involves more than just showing up," Fr. Dave said. "My Protestant friends like to say that sitting in a church doesn't make you a Christian any more than standing in your garage makes you a car. It's just like what St. Augustine wrote: "God has many the church doesn't have and the church has many that God doesn't have."

"Their points are the same: mere membership and attendance won't do," he told me. "God is not fooled by appearances. Your life has to be transformed by Jesus Christ living and operating in and through you, and that's not a spectator sport, Tim."

Then he told me a story about another person who'd wondered about what the future would hold. "Once upon a time," Fr. Dave said, "there was a lovely young lady here named Terri, who was in the same program as you're in. She had no trouble making friends, and lots of young men were interested in her."

"As time progressed, she'd narrowed the field to two of them, George and Tony. Both were good men, I thought," Fr. Dave continued, "but very different from each other."

"You wouldn't pick George out as anything special. He was kind of ordinary-looking and his social skills were — hmm, how shall we say it? — 'primitive' would be a charitable way to phrase it."

"Tony, on the other hand, was a fraternity man, the captain of the football team, and president of the student council. He knew how to work a crowd; had plenty of charisma, and always seemed to get whatever he wanted when he wanted it."

"One thing I knew he wanted was Terri. I don't mean that in an ugly way," Fr. Dave said, "He just wanted other people to notice him with this fabulous young lady on his arm."

"One day Terri stopped by after mass and asked me if we could talk. I said 'Sure!' She wanted me to help her sort out her feelings for George and Tony. 'Both of them treat me well, and I like them,' she said, 'but they're so different.' I asked her to tell me about it."

"'It's exciting to be around Tony,' Terri said, 'but I can't help getting the feeling that even though he likes having me around he doesn't seem to want to get to know me as a person.'"

"'George isn't a Tony and never will be,' Terri said, 'but he's kind and gentle. He wants to find out everything he can about me and he wants me to know him. He has this way of just inviting me to share his life, and he's genuinely delighted when I invite him to share mine.'"

"I asked Terri whether she preferred to be excited or to be loved; whether association with a popular person was more valuable to her than a relationship with a person who might just want to know her and love her for who she was."

"'Who works harder at getting to know you?' I asked her, and I could see her thinking about that. 'No question, Father Dave,' Terri said, 'George — he kind of has to — being open and relaxed with people comes hard for him; but he wants to, especially with me."

"Everything's effortless for Tony, compared to George. Sometimes it seems as if it's all too easy for him and I wonder sometimes if he's sincere.' Terri got quiet for a while and then she asked me, 'How can I get a hint that I'm making the right choice, Fr. Dave?'"

"'Maybe it's like getting hints about whether you're saved or not,' I told her. 'Perhaps it's only at the end that you know for sure,' I told her. 'There are hints all along though, Terri. Take a close look.'"

"'What God offers each of us is a relationship, Terri, not just a casual association. Each relationship unfolds as we live our lives with God. Each one is a unique and fabulous story of deep love and endless discovery of ever more wonderful dimensions of you and the God who loves you, entwined in a dance that never ends. God doesn't want to collect arm candy — God wants to love us."

"What kind of stories are your two friends writing with you?

Which one is transforming you through the lived experience of love? Take a look, Terri,' I told her, 'those stories contain all the hints you'll ever need.'"

Fr. Dave stopped and looked at me. "It's the same with you, Tim. Do you dream that you can know the ending of a story that's still being written? Forget the meatballs during Lent when you were nine. Look at your faith as it's unfolding right now."

"If you want a hint about whether you'll be saved or not, just ask yourself: 'Is the tale of my life unfolding as a story of the transforming love of Jesus Christ or is it a more like a book report about someone else's story?'"

"Remember, God isn't fooled by appearances. In your response," Fr. Dave told me, "you'll find the only real hint you'll ever get along the way, and the only one you'll ever need."

Alice And The Bean

Alice asked her father one day why they always had to go to mass on Sunday.

"We all get together to celebrate the fabulous gift that God gave to us," Dad explained.

"What gift?" Alice wanted to know.

"The gift of himself," Dad said, "The gift that bridges what it means to be a human person and what it means to be God."

"Why can't we just celebrate that right here?" Alice asked. "Why do we have to go to church?"

"It's like the way it is at a birthday party," Dad said. "You have to go where it says to go on the invitation. That's where the cake and soda are."

"Think about it. Suppose you had a birthday, invited all your friends and no one showed up for the party. Then suppose you went around the next day and found out that each one of them had privately celebrated your birthday at home without you?"

"That would be weird, Dad," Alice said.

"I think so too, but there are folks who do just that," Dad said.

Alice thought about it for a moment.

"But mass isn't a birthday party, Dad," Alice objected.

"In a way it is, Alice," Dad said. "We celebrate our birth into a whole new relationship with God that we get to experience through Christ in the Eucharist."

"I never feel any different," Alice said. "I usually come out of mass feeling the same as I did when I went in."

Dad wondered how to respond to Alice and said a little prayer. Then it came to him, the way things can come to us when we pray like that.

"Follow me," Dad said, and he and Alice went out to the garden pile in the garage.

Dad looked around for a bit, and then took out a small pot, a few bean seeds and some potting soil. He put the soil in the pot and gave a bean seed to Alice.

"Okay Alice, first take a good look at the seed and then plant it in the pot."

Alice gave the seed a keen once-over and then planted it.

Dad closed his eyes, counted to three, and then said to Alice "Okay, that's long enough. Now, dig it up."

"I just planted it," Alice said.

"I know," Dad replied.

Alice gave her Dad a dubious look, but then dug up the seed.

"What does it look like?" Dad asked.

"It hasn't changed at all, Dad," Alice said. "It looks the same as when I put it in."

"Just the way you look the same before mass and after you come out?" Dad asked.

Alice laughed.

"If we leave the seed there long enough, water it, and give it fertilizer, it'll eventually turn into a plant full of beans, right?" Dad asked.

"Sure it will, Dad," Alice agreed. "It needs time." "So you're saying it's like that with me and mass too, right?"

"Right," Dad said. "If we put you in God's garden, water you with prayer and fertilize you with the Eucharist, let the sunlight of love shine on you and spray you with care if harmful bugs come along, eventually you'll bear fabulous fruit. You need time too."

"And then God will eat me up?" Alice asked with a raised eyebrow.

"Not exactly," Dad said, "but in some way, like the way things we eat become our body, so we too will become what God is, after we've finished growing here — and we have it on God's own word that it will be good."

"Thanks, Dad," Alice said. "That helps me think about it in a different way."

The Maltese Falcon

A few years ago I went to a business meeting and the speaker told us a true story about his family and *The Maltese Falcon*. His dad, it seems, was a big fan of Humphrey Bogart and loved all his films, but his deepest affection was for *The Maltese Falcon.*

In case you've forgotten or never knew, the Maltese Falcon was a small hollow statue in which a fortune in gems had been hidden.

One day his family had stopped at a tag sale down in Pennsylvania while they were on vacation. His dad noticed a small statue of the Maltese Falcon on sale for $5 and decided to pick it up, much against the wishes of his mom, who said the house already had enough Bogart memorabilia in it for a museum.

The statue stood for years on the piano in the living room. Kids played with it. It got knocked down, almost thrown away by mom on various occasions, and was used as an ash tray by smokers who came to visit.

One day there was an ad in the Daily News that Sotheby's was having an open house, at which anyone who thought they had anything of value could bring it in and have it appraised for free. The speaker and his siblings decided to have some fun and badgered their dad into taking the statue of the Maltese Falcon there.

He was a good sport, so he played along to share in the fun. There was a huge line, but when his turn came, Dad handed the statue to the expert, who took a careful look at it and then at Dad.

He told him: "This is amazing. Only two of these were ever made. One's at a museum in Hollywood and the other was lost somehow, but you've found it. I'll give you $50,000 for it." It was hard to tell who was more astonished, Dad or the kids. Who would've ever thought this crummy statue had been worth $50,000 all along?

The auctioneer smiled, shook his head and said "I wonder how many other treasures you have whose value you never appreciated?"

Dad took a look at the auctioneer, and then at his family, and they looked back at him. "You've got a point there," he said. "I think I'll be paying even more attention to my family." The auctioneer gave Dad a puzzled look, but his family lit up like a Christmas tree. In that moment, they knew that there's no price on a treasure like their father's love.

The Shield

Every good mom and dad wants to make sure that their children know they're good and valuable, and from where their worth comes. When their daughter, Terry, sat at the dinner table looking sadder than she usually did, Mom and Dad glanced at each other and wordlessly decided to build their daughter up.

"You know that Dad and I love you, Terry," Mom said.

"Yeah, I know that," Terry said, "but sometimes, when I think about myself, I don't like what I see; especially when I'm being bullied."

Mom and Dad heard that last part loud and clear. They knew they had to give Terry a chance to talk about it.

"How do you feel when that happens?" Mom asked.

"Very sad," Terry said. "I get angry, and then I get sad, and then I want to hide or not even go to school anymore. I feel like I'm no good when everyone puts me down."

"What do you suppose makes people think they're good?" Mom asked.

Terry thought about that for a moment or two. "When other people like you and Dad and anyone else who loves me tells me so, I guess," Terry said. "But not everybody loves me; some kids hate me."

"Let's explore that, Terry," her Dad said. "Suppose the people who hate you weren't there. Would you still feel you were no good?"

"I guess not," Terry said. "But other people like them would probably come along soon enough. I wish everyone just loved me like you and Mom do."

"I think you're finding that life's not like that, Terry," Dad said. "Everyone's in a different spot in their journey through life, and some haven't embraced the law of love yet. Some perhaps never will. Do you really want to hand over control of your sense of self-worth to the hands of people who haven't learned to love?"

"That doesn't sound like a good idea, Dad," Terry said, "but how can I avoid those people — they're right in my face."

"You can't avoid them," Dad said, "but you do have a shield that no one can ever get through, no matter how hard they try."

"What's that?" Terry wanted to know.

"We'll get there," Dad said with a smile. "Let's talk some more first."

"Why else do you think people think they're worth something?" Mom asked.

"Well, everyone thinks they're good at something," Terry said. "I'm good at soccer and softball. You have to be good at something before you can feel good about yourself, don't you?"

"Do you really think that's true, Terry?" Dad said. "Maybe God delights in everyone for some other reason, whether they can do something well or not. Think about Uncle Fred. He lost both of his legs in Vietnam, but he's still worth something, don't you think?"

"Oh, yeah," Terry said, "Uncle Fred. He can't do much anymore but he's probably the happiest guy I know. I think he's happy just to be alive."

Mom and Dad nodded silently.

"What else do people do to make them think they're worth something?" Mom asked again.

"Some kids act like they're Zeus," Terry said, "They push everyone around and force them to do what they want. And if you don't see it their way they come down hard on you and say stuff behind your back. They want to feel powerful and they make you think you're only worth something if you do what they say."

"Do you think that's true?" Mom asked.

"No," Terry said. "They're afraid or angry or something. They aren't happy. I don't think they know much about God."

"That's a pretty keen insight, Terry," her Mom said, and Dad nodded in agreement.

"People have value even if they don't have power," Dad said. "And of course, they've got the shield."

"You keep on going on about a shield, Dad" Terry scowled. "Are you going to tell me about that or not?"

"Soon," Dad promised. "But first tell me more about how people measure their value."

"There are some kids who think they're perfect," Terry said. "They don't swear, cheat, lie, or steal. But when they do, everyone thinks it's pretty funny. Everyone except them, of course."

"Do you think it's funny?" Dad asked. Terry squirmed a bit and said "Well, sometimes I laugh, but not really, Dad. I feel kind of sad for them because they only think they're worth something if they're perfect. When they mess up they take it hard."

Mom and Dad nodded in agreement again, happily impressed with their daughter's growing wisdom.

"Why else do people feel they're valuable?" Mom asked.

"Well, we have the sport jocks and the beauty queens," Terry said, looking down. "They rub it in your face that you're not them; that you're not in their crowd. Not all of them, but some of them do."

"What do you think they'll look like when they're 89?" Dad asked with a smile.

"You're weird, Dad," Terry said. "I guess they'll look like you!"

Mom intervened quickly and said, "Your father's just telling you that it's great to feel good about what you look like or can do, but it's probably not a good idea to base your self-worth on that. Strength and beauty are gone before you know it. If you peg your self-worth on that, you can end up pretty miserable when your body changes. Trust me on that," Mom said with a wry smile.

"If my self-worth doesn't come from other people's liking me, or what I can do, or what I look like, or who I can influence or how well I behave then what does it come from?" Terry asked, exasperated.

"Let me tell you the truth, Terry," Dad said, "We're priceless simply because we're each unique expressions of God's love: each of us is a person who can love and can be loved. That's the rock-solid, unmovable foundation of our value as people, and it comes from God directly and unconditionally. No one can ever say or do anything that can make you or me a person who cannot love or a person who cannot be loved."

It got quiet in the room for a bit. Then Terry asked: "Is that the shield, Dad?"

"Yes, Terry," Dad said "The shield is nothing less than the awareness of the presence of God, who is love deeply wrapped within and around us. The bully hasn't been born who can get past it."

The Check

Once upon a time there was a little boy in a small town not too far from here who greeted his type-A, workaholic father as he returned home from work one day with a question: "Dad, how much do you make an hour?"

His dad was astonished and said, "Look, son, I don't even tell your mother how much I make. Don't bother me now, I just got home from work and I'm tired. Go watch TV."

But his son didn't give up. "Dad, please just tell me. Please — it's important — how much do you make an hour?" To get rid of his son, his father just scowled and said, "Twenty dollars."

Well, his son wasn't quite done with him. "Okay, Dad," he said, "Could you loan me ten dollars?" At that, his Dad blew up and yelled at him, "Is that why you wanted to know? So you could figure out how much you could get out of me?" The rest of his tirade isn't worth repeating except to say that the little boy was sent to bed crying and without supper.

Over dinner, his wife suggested just a bit fearfully that perhaps he had been too tough with their son. Maybe his son needed the money for school or to buy something. Her husband wasn't hearing a bar of that song, but his wife continued, trying to convince him of their son's innocence, and Dad began to feel a little guilty.

After dinner he went and watched TV by himself for awhile, but his wife's words bothered him. His conscience wouldn't let him rest and he finally decided to go to his son's room, give him the money and find out why he needed it.

So up he went and asked, "Are you asleep?"

"No, Dad. Why?" his son said.

"I thought about it some more. Here's the money you asked for earlier," his Dad said, throwing some cash on his son's bed.

"Thanks, Dad!" his son said, eagerly taking the money. Then he reached under his pillow and took out some more money — mostly crumpled dollar bills and small change.

He handed it to his father and said "Now I have enough!"

"Enough for what?" his Dad asked.

"Now I have twenty dollars!" he said to his father. He looked up at his Dad with wide, hopeful eyes and asked: "Dad — can I buy an hour of your time?"

His dad was stunned.

"You want to buy an hour of my time?"

"Sure, Dad," his son said with a hopeful look on his face. "All I want to do is have an hour to play together with you and laugh and talk — just you and me — and this way you won't lose any money because of me."

His dad covered his eyes, excused himself quickly, got up, and told his son he'd be right back. It took a short while before he could recover from what his son had told him.

Then he went downstairs and told his wife what had happened. She began to cry, too. Together they decided what to do next. Dad went to his desk, took out their checkbook and wrote out a check to his son. There was no amount. The date said 'Anytime,' and it was signed simply, 'Dad.'

Then he went back into his son's room, handed him the check and explained what it was. "You don't have to pay me, son," Dad said. "I can see now that I'd gotten lost in myself and my work. I forgot what a father's real business is in life, but you reminded me. I'm giving you this special check. Whenever you need time from me and I tell you I'm too busy, just show me this check and I promise I'll give you all the time you need."[2]

2   The part about buying an hour of his father's time is not original (anonymously received from the email world), but the part about the check is original with this story.

Tomás

Phil and Barbara adopted a Colombian child many years ago. It was a big and expensive deal, but one day baby Tomás boarded the plane in Bogotá and came home with them. Years passed and, if you knew them, you'd agree with me that Phil and Barbara were the best parents little Tomás could ever have asked for. He always knew that he was loved because Phil and Barbara never stopped showing him by their words and care for him that it was truly so.

Like many adoptive children, as he grew up, little Tomás became curious about where he had come from. Phil and Barbara had made a scrapbook that had pictures, newspaper articles and, somewhat against the rules, letters written by Tomás' family and neighbors in Colombia back then. Carefully keeping it up to date, they had on hand just what Tomás needed to know when he came of an age.

The evening he asked about it, Phil and Barbara took out the scrapbook and gently placed it on Tomás' lap. The scrapbook began with Tomás' birth and a letter from his Mom saying that her husband had abandoned them and that neither she nor anyone in her family had the resources to raise him. They had put him up for adoption, hoping for a better life for him.

Pictures and news clippings from that time filled in Tomás' curiosity. Then came the hard part. The scrapbook began to tell the tale of the unrest that grew in Colombia over time. It described a time of terror: death squads, unimaginable suffering, and violence.

Then, on the last page, it described the year the villages in his region had been destroyed. The scrapbook didn't say whether his family had been killed. It didn't have to — the pictures said it all.

Tomás stared at those pages for a long time. Then he looked up at Phil and Barbara and said "If you hadn't come to save me, I would be dead."

Phil and Barbara nodded — yes, that was so. Then Barbara got up, took their crucifix down from the wall and laid it on top of the scrapbook. "Our story's just like this one, Tomás. If Jesus hadn't come to save us, we'd ALL be dead. When we adopted you, we were simply doing for you something like what Jesus did for all of us. You're in our family now, and loved, and as safe as we can make you. We're in Jesus' family too, and loved, and as safe as he can make us; and that's as safe as it gets. There is nothing to fear in this world or the next."

Then Barbara looked intently at Tomás and asked, "Tell me Tomás — do you believe that?"

Tomás didn't answer immediately. After a few minutes, the reality of what had happened to him, what had happened to his family and what Barbara was telling him about Jesus slowly sank in.

He looked at the tears in her eyes through the tears in his own. "Yes," he said.

Barbara smiled, gave him a big hug and said, "Tomás, promise me then that you'll never forget what's been done for you and what's been done for all of us."

The Mercy Of Baseball

There was a story on ESPN[3] a while ago that might help explain the quality of mercy. It was about a young lady named Sara Tucholsky, who played softball for Central Washington in the Great Northwest Conference. She was a solid player, but had never hit a home run.

Her team was playing Western Oregon that day in April, the second game of a double-header, and they were behind 2-0. It was the top of the second and two of her teammates were on base. With a 3 and 2 count she saw the most perfect pitch she'd ever seen in her life come her way. She swung at the ball with all her might and sent it sailing over the fence.

Her team erupted with joy, but as they greeted the runners driven home they looked around for Sara and saw that she wasn't rounding the bases. Sara had indeed come around first, but realized she hadn't touched base. She had turned around quickly to do that, but somehow her leg didn't pivot quite right and she had fallen to the ground in terrible pain. She had torn a ligament in her knee and couldn't move.

The coaches rushed to her, but she couldn't even stand up. They asked the ump what could be done but the rules were clear. If she didn't round the bases and touch them all, she would not have her home run, even though the ball had gone over the fence. Sorry, that was the rule. No mercy.

Could they help her around the bases? Nope — if they even touched her, she'd be out. No mercy. So, no home run? Sorry, the rules say you could put in a runner, but it'd only be a double then. No mercy.

Just then something amazing happened. As everyone was talking, the women on the other team learned that this would have been Sara's first home run. It didn't take long for them to realize it would probably also be her last, and they all decided what they would do.

3   Viewable on youtube at http://youtube.com/watchtv=ttkBP2XDZve

Two of them went up to the ump and asked, "How about if *we* carry her around the bases?" The ump was stunned — *this* had never happened before. He checked the rules, but there was no rule about the opposing team doing something like that. It seems that when it comes to mercy, there are no rules.

"You can do that," the ump said. "But if you do, you may lose the game."

They simply asked, "Will her home run count?"

"Yes," the ump said. "It'll count."

He knew, they knew, and you have probably already figured out what would happen next.

Mallory Holtman and her teammate, Liz Wallace, gently picked up Sara in their arms and carried her around the bases, bending together to lower her gently so that Sara could touch each base. When they reached home, the three girls looked up, expecting to see people laughing at them and shaking their heads, but that's not what they saw. There wasn't a dry eye in the ball-park, not even the ump's. Mercy and compassion, not the rules, were victorious that day.

Monsters Under The Bed

There was a young family of five in a small town not too far from here — Mom, Dad and three small children. One day Mom announced to the family at dinner that her mom, who lived in California by herself, was going to have a fairly significant operation and would need care at home for a while. She was going to travel out there for a few weeks to keep her company and arrange for longer term care.

The children had lots of questions, like "Who was going to take care of them?" and "when would she be back?" and "was grandma going to be okay?" Mom and Dad did their best to reassure the children that Dad would take care of them while Mom was away and that everything was going to be all right.

And so it came to pass that Mom left to take care of *her* mother. Dad and the kids did pretty well for a while, but one night the youngest, Terry, came downstairs from her room after Dad had said their prayers with them and put them all to bed.

Dad was reading a book and enjoying a cup of tea and was surprised to see little Terry.

"What's the matter Terry — can't sleep?" Dad asked.

"No," Terry told him, "I'm afraid to go to sleep."

"Afraid of what?" Dad asked.

"The monster under my bed," Terry told him.

Dad was tempted to tell her that monsters didn't exist, but then he realized it would be better to take his daughter seriously, so he closed his book, put down his tea and told her there hadn't been monsters in the house for a long time now, so they had better go check.

"Is it the green, slimy kind or the furry sort?" Dad asked, taking a flashlight from the kitchen and heading upstairs with Terry.

"I don't know," Terry said. "I ran out of my room before I could see."

When they got upstairs, Dad shone the light under the bed and sure enough, there were no monsters.

"Looks like it went away, Terry," Dad said.

"It'll be back," Terry said, "as soon as you go away."

Dad thought he knew what was happening, so he sat down with Terry and said "You know, you're right — it's probably just hiding here, somewhere else in the room. But you know, most monsters are just afraid of something themselves — they're not really mean at all. They usually just want someone to listen to them. Maybe that's all it wants."

Terry wasn't sure it was a good idea to talk with monsters, but Dad said, "Let's take a risk and ask it what it wants to tell us."

So they sat there quietly for a short while.

Then Terry said, "I think it's lonely. I think it misses its mom."

Dad told Terry to tell the monster out loud that it could still love its mom even though she wasn't around. Moms live inside our hearts as well as outside where we can see and touch them.

Terry did that but then looked her dad in the eye and said, "The monster is afraid that it will never see its mom again."

Dad nodded and then said, "What should we tell the monster, Terry?"

Terry thought about it for a few moments and then said, "You have to trust that you will see your Mom again."

Dad agreed that was a pretty good answer. It was kind of like the way we all trust that we'll see Jesus some day.

They sat there together quietly and said their prayers again. Then Dad gave Terry a kiss, tucked her in, and turned off the light. Terry didn't come downstairs again; seems that the monster had gone away.

Sandwiches

Many years ago I used to work in lower Manhattan. I'd take the subway in from my apartment in Queens and walk a few blocks to work. There were always homeless folks around, but at that time in my life I never paid much attention to them.

One day I happened to be standing next to a guy in the subway who was carrying a shopping bag. All of us around him could smell peanut butter. I looked down into the shopping bag and saw that it was full of peanut butter sandwiches — must've been forty of fifty, at least. He saw me looking at them, our eyes met, and I remarked to him that that was quite a lunch he'd packed for himself.

He laughed and said that the sandwiches weren't for him. I asked if they were for the rest of us in the subway car, but he just laughed again and said "no." Then he gave me a piercing yet friendly look and invited me to follow him and he'd show me.

I glanced at my watch and saw that I had a few extra minutes, so I said "okay." When we got down to South Ferry we walked out of the subway and up into the open together. Some homeless folks were at the top of the stairs, waiting for him.

I felt uncomfortable, but he started to greet them by name and began to hand out the peanut butter sandwiches.

As we walked down the street, other people came up along with folks he already knew. He'd ask who they were, and then give them a sandwich and a smile, always using their names as he did so.

The shopping bag was empty inside of two blocks. I was awe-struck. I asked him why he did this.

"One day," he told me, "I came out of the subway and a homeless woman asked me for some money. I got angry because I thought she was just going to use it on alcohol, so I barked at her 'What do *you* need money for?' She simply looked at me and said, 'I'm hungry.'"

"I pulled away from her brusquely, but the hurt look on her face lingered within me as I walked away. Then I thought about my own abundance.

I wasn't hungry. *I* had money in *my* wallet. Nobody had ever barked at *me* the way I'd barked at her. I turned around to see if I could find the homeless woman again but she was gone, lost in the rush-hour crowds of downtown Manhattan."

"Aside from the bitterness I'd felt towards myself at having treated another human being like that, I felt a kind of hunger well up within me; a hunger to make amends somehow, to repent of that way of treating people."

"When I arrived at work, I walked down the aisle toward my office and noticed a cornucopia full of candy sitting on my secretary's desk. I grabbed a piece and began to think as I unwrapped it. Something about me needed to become like that cornucopia. By the end of the day I knew exactly what I was going to do."

"At first it was just a couple of sandwiches, but as word got around the office, other people began to give me money, jars of peanut butter, and bread. There are a couple of us doing this now," he said. "None of us thinks we're a big deal. We're just a drop in the bucket. God's the big deal. I hope one day I'll run into that homeless woman again. I need to thank her for feeding me."

Emily

Throughout history, God has always provided a way for us to be healed when we've acknowledged that we've done what's wrong. God's all about life, not death; salvation, not destruction.

The images in stories that talk about this, like that Bible passage in which God tells Moses to hold up a snake, might make it seem as if God's using magic as a means of healing with that bronze snake. Likewise, comparing a bronze snake to Jesus might strike us as being something of a stretch.

Let's take a closer look at that bronze snake on a pole. It's an ancient symbol, and it appears in many cultures, including our own. The earliest images we have of it are around five thousand years old. Sometimes people associate a single snake on a pole with the caduceus, or the wand of Hermes. But they're wrong: a caduceus actually has *two* snakes wound around a pole.

Since the mid-nineteenth century the wand of Hermes has been a symbol of the medical profession, and hence a symbol of healing. This is kind of unfortunate, since in Greek mythology Hermes also happened to be the guide of the dead and protector of gamblers, liars, and thieves — not the kinds of associations one would voluntarily prefer to make with the healing profession. Frankly speaking, somebody goofed.[4]

The pharmacists have got it right, though. They have a single snake around a pole. This thing is called the Rod of Asclepius, who happened to be a physician in the mythology of ancient Greece. It, too, is a symbol of healing.[5]

There you have it: right and wrong. But how then do we connect these snake symbols to the cross?

To grasp the connection, and what kind of healing God does for us through Jesus and the cross, we first have to understand the sickness. To find out what the sickness is, let's have some fun and do a little detective work together. To start, we'll look at the clues. We have a stick, which is part of a tree, and a snake.

4   https://en.wikipedia.org/wiki/Caduceus
5   https://en.wikipedia.org/wiki/Rod_of_Asclepius

Let's drop the Greek mythology for a moment and look at this symbol with the eyes of our faith. When was the first time in the Bible that a tree and a snake appeared together? If you're thinking of the Garden of Eden, you're right! The griping the Israelites were doing in the desert is an extension of what was going on in the Garden of Eden.

Just as Adam and Eve wanted things their way, so the Israelites in the desert wanted things their own way: they were through with following God. The sickness — what's in us that needs healing — is that dimension of human nature that rebels against God, and refuses to trust in his care.

Saint Paul once asked — "From whence comes this evil?" St. Augustine answered with the doctrine of original sin: there's something shrouded in the origin and history of humanity that makes disobedience and rebellion appealing to us. What God heals with the bronze snake and what God heals through Jesus is this alienation from God, this separation, or sin, that's so deeply rooted in humanity's origins.

One of the themes of the snake story is that the consequences of sin and rebellion are like a snakebite — painful and potentially fatal if not treated promptly. You have to know what to do when you're bitten, and have a way to be healed.

As I read this, I reflected on my snakebite training in the Army. If you've been in the military, you probably know it by heart, too. Step one is "remain calm." That rule could not possibly have been written by anyone who'd ever been bitten by a real snake, but there it is: Don't panic. That's good advice for sinners like us, too. Don't panic — the love and compassion of God runs deep.

The next step was to kill the snake, but without damaging its head. It was left to our imagination how actually to do that, but it was an important thing, we were told, because the head was needed to be able to identify the snake so that we could be treated properly and healed. It's like that with us sinners, too. We have to be able to name our sin to be able to deal with it and be healed, and it doesn't help to make them unrecognizable.

There is something else about the snakebite we call sin. It is something not covered in the Army field manual. Now I've never been bitten by a snake, but somehow I can't imagine anyone who has been bitten by a snake denying that they've been bitten. Yet when it comes to sin and rebellion in everyday life, we do that all the time.

Let me tell you a story that shows this in action. A little girl named Emily was sitting at the dinner table in front of a plate full of carrots and peas — something like that disgusting food the Israelites were complaining about.

Her dad told her she'd only get dessert if she ate all her carrots and peas. You could tell from the expression on her face that she wasn't too happy about that. Then he told her he was leaving for a few minutes and would be back soon. What Emily didn't know was that her father was secretly videotaping her.

As soon as her dad left, little Emily stretched her neck to see and make sure her dad wasn't around. Then she took the plate of carrots and peas, dumped them in the trash and put the plate back on the table.

When her dad returned she pretended to finish chewing and swallowing the last carrot and pea. Her dad asked, "Did you finish your carrots and peas, Emily?"

"Yeesss," she said, not looking him in the eye.

"Are you sure?" her Dad asked.

"Yeesss," Emily said again.

"You didn't throw them in the trash, did you?"

"Noooo."

Then they looked at the video together. Her dad asked if that was her in the video.

To his utter astonishment she said "No!"

"Well it sure looks like you!" her dad exclaimed. "If it isn't you, then who is it?"

"That's the *bad* Emily," his daughter told him.

And so indeed it was: original sin — our shadow side — the part of us we do not like to admit even exists — the part that contradicts our preferred view of ourselves — there it was, captured live on video. Saint Augustine would've loved it.

Let's connect the dots now. The first step in healing, is indeed to remain calm and recognize our sinful and rebellious nature, but confident of the love and compassion of God. The next step is to let God destroy that sinful inclination within us — to be healed, not by staring at a bronze serpent, but by looking instead at the cross of Jesus Christ.

Jesus is the way God provides for us to be healed when we acknowledge that we've done what's wrong. Saint Paul tells us that Jesus became sin for our sake. Look at the cross — that's what sin does to a human being. It immobilizes us in loneliness, humiliation, pain, and eventually death. Stare at the cross and know sin.

Stare at the cross and know too that it is precisely this that God transforms within us into the joy of everlasting life, through the power of the resurrection of Jesus, alive within you and me. For "God did not send the Son into the world to condemn the world, but...that the world might be saved through him" (John 3:16).

Vinnie And The AC

Vinnie worked in a factory up in Massachusetts. Last summer, when it was pretty hot and humid, a co-worker came up to Vinnie and told him he had gotten hold of some air conditioners. Good ones — 15,000 BTUs. "Like a refrigerator," he said.

"Man, I could use an air conditioner," Vinnie said, "but I haven't got much money."

"These are cheap, Vinnie," his friend told him.

"How cheap?" Vinnie wanted to know.

"$50," his friend said.

"Fifty bucks!" Vinnie exclaimed. "Where'd you get them?"

"Vinnie," his co-worker said, "All you gotta know is they're $50. Do you care what truck they fell off?"

Vinnie thought about it for a moment. It didn't feel right, but he was hot and now he could get cool on the cheap. And hey, if he didn't buy one someone else would. Whoever owned these things wasn't ever going to see them again anyway. Then he reached for his wallet and gave his co-worker $50 in cash.

"Pick it up at my house this evening," said his friend, taking the cash.

"Okay," Vinnie said.

The rest of the day, Vinnie tried to concentrate on his work, but he couldn't. All that went through his mind was what his mom and dad used to tell him about the worth of hard work and how bad it was to steal. This wasn't really stealing, Vinnie tried to say to himself. Someone else stole the air conditioners, not him!

"Good thinking, son," his dad's voice said inside him. "All you're doing is paying someone else to do your stealing for you."

Vinnie spent the rest of the day stewing in a crisis of conscience.

Work ended. The sun went down and came up again. Vinnie went back to work. He had made his decision.

"Hey Vinnie," his co-worker said, jabbing him in the side, "I told you to show up at my place and get your air conditioner."

"I don't want it," Vinnie said.

"Are you crazy?" his friend said. "A/C for $50. What, are you — stupid?"

"I don't want it," Vinnie repeated.

"Yes you do," his friend snarled. "What are you all of a sudden, some kind of saint?"

"Yeah, that's it — a saint," Vinnie shot back.

"Don't kid yourself, Vinnie," his friend said. "You're just like the rest of us. And now you want your money back too, right, jerk?"

"Keep it," Vinnie said. "You can go give it to the poor. Oh, excuse me, you already have it."

The conversation after this point isn't fit for church, so we'll leave Vinnie and his friend for now and let them cool off a bit.

Rocky

My friend, Ted, told me a story about the kids he used to hang with when he was growing up. One of them, Rocky, was one of those natural leaders. He was the guy who came up with the games they'd play or the places they'd go. In school he was always the captain of the team, the class president, the one who got picked by teachers to organize things and so on. He also wore his religion like a badge.

His aunt had given him a gold crucifix when he was young, and Ted said he couldn't remember a time when Rocky wasn't wearing it. In Rocky's family religion went deep, but they all bore it lightly, as if it were the most natural thing in the world, as it is.

Everyone in their little group of friends went to mass because, well, Rocky went to mass. Rocky believed. He seemed to have this special relationship with Jesus, and he didn't mind talking about it. To Ted and his friends, Rocky got his strength and courage from Jesus. They figured if Jesus was good enough for him, Jesus was good enough for them, too.

After graduation, they'd all gone their separate ways, but stayed in touch. Rocky got an appointment to West Point, and graduated near the top of his class. He was sent to Vietnam, to command a company of Rangers.

After only a few months, the letters from overseas stopped coming, and shortly thereafter Rocky's family was told that he was dead. He'd been shot helping a wounded Ranger get on a medevac helicopter during a fierce fire fight near Hill 407 in Quang Tri province. All that was left now was his story and the gold crucifix.

Ted and his friends attended the funeral mass. Rocky's aunt gave Ted the gold crucifix and said that Rocky had told her he wanted him to have it in case anything happened, to remind both him and their old friends from the neighborhood that even though someone might be able to kill him, nothing can kill our faith. Ted took it out from under his shirt and showed it to me. He says he can't remember a day he hasn't worn it since then.

Tommy And John

There's a story about little Tommy, who asked his mom if he could have his friend John over to play. Mom said sure, and when John arrived she brought them some cookies and milk. John looked surprised — "Are they for us?" he asked. "Of course!" Tommy said, "My mom loves us." John looked surprised, but he didn't say anything.

After Mom left, Tommy took out some paper and crayons.

"What are you making?" John wanted to know.

"I'm making a thank-you card for my mom," Tommy explained.

"What for?" John asked, "Just because we got some cookies?"

"I only want to say 'thanks' and 'I love you,' to my mom" Tommy told him. "My dad does that a lot and Mom always seems to like it."

John was silent. Then he said "We don't do anything like that in our family."

As it started to get dark, Tommy asked his mom, if he could invite John to stay for dinner. John called home and his mom said she didn't care. Tommy's dad came home from work and there was lots of noisy conversation, laughter, and hugs. Tommy's dad welcomed John into the family's glow and helped him join the conversation.

When they sat down to eat, they asked John if he wanted to say grace. "What's that?" John asked.

Tommy's dad smiled and said, "It's a way to say 'thank you' to God for all the good things we've been given, like the food we get to eat."

"I don't know how to do that," John said. "We've never done anything like that in our family."

"Let me show you how it goes," Dad said. "You can join us if you feel comfortable." Tommy's dad said grace, and everyone else chimed in with their own personal thanks. When it was John's turn, they gently invited him to say something too, if he wanted.

"I'm not sure who God is," John said, "but if he's anything like the people in this family, I'd be real glad to meet him."

The Calling

There's a story in the Bible about young Samuel that tells us what the process of becoming aware of God is like. Samuel starts off asleep, and is awakened by God. He remains present to God, but he doesn't take the next step until his mentor Eli tells him that merely being present to God is not enough.

Eli instructs him to *listen* to God. After he learns to listen, he becomes an effective prophet — a person called by God through whom God can call others. That's the process — unawareness to awareness — that eventually leads us to active listening and to the full release of who and what we are in the service of God.

It's like the story about Bill and Alice. Bill was a cradle Catholic who had been an altar boy, went to Catholic schools and graduated from a Catholic college. He had spent a lot of time reading and studying, trying to discover what it was that God wanted him to do. Bill felt that even with all his education and his Catholic background, he knew a lot *about* God, but wasn't so sure he could honestly say he knew God the way you'd say you know a person.

Like many of us, his faith varied in intensity. There were periods of time where he'd gone to mass more out of habit than conviction. It bothered him that he was doing all the right stuff, but had never been gripped by the Lord the way you're swept off your feet by someone you love.

That all changed when he met Alice, the woman who was to become his wife. He was delighted by her sheer joy in the wonder of creation and the rich, uncomplicated relationship she had with God. He wanted what she had — in his heart he knew for sure that what she had was what he was looking for.

One Sunday they had gone to mass together and were walking in Central Park afterward. Alice asked Bill if he knew what it meant to be called. Bill proceeded to tell her at length about all his studies and things he'd read.

When he paused to take a breath, she asked "Have you ever stopped to listen?"

He asked her what she meant.

"If I want to get to know people," Alice said, "I let them 'come and see,' the way Jesus said. Everything we've done since we've known each other has been to go deeper into that invitation to 'come and see,' Bill. I've followed and mostly listened and seen who you are."

"Have you done the same with me? I hope so, because I have this strange feeling that your life and mine are entwined in the depths of the love of God somehow. When we received communion together at mass this morning I heard an urgent call to connect with something lovely and good, and way bigger than you or me. I think God wants me to experience the joy of His presence and be a way other people, especially you, can come to experience it too."

Bill stopped, looked into her eyes and asked, "Are you saying you're my calling?"

Alice looked back at him, smiled and said "Are you asking me to be?"

Bill burst out in the kind of laughter we all have when we're surprised by getting exactly what we need and want, and said "Of course!" Alice gave him the kind of hug that told him everything he had to know about what she thought of that response.

I tell you this story because in the end God's call to us is more than a job, more than a career, more even than an awakening like Samuel's. God's call to us, you see, is a love story.

Tim At IBM

Many years ago I worked at a consulting unit within IBM in Connecticut and upstate NY as the regional large system specialist. Part of the job was to help people get the most out of their mainframe systems, but often I had to drop everything and go fix other peoples' messes.

When that happened I found, more often than not, that the job boiled down to sorting through the wreckage created by folks who didn't have much experience, but didn't believe that, and who'd plowed ahead anyway, doing what they'd thought was the right thing to do.

I'm sure other people who fix things have seen plenty of this, too. Is there an electrician who hasn't had to fix the light switches that suddenly don't work anymore after some "genius" has worked on them, or a mechanic who hasn't listened in silent disbelief to people's astonishing stories of how they "fixed" their cars? They too know the truth of what Mark Twain's friend Artemus Ward had said: "It ain't what we don't know that gets us into trouble — it's what we think we know that just ain't so."[6]

Fixer-uppers also know that the first thing many folks who have made a mess of it will try to do, unless they 'fess up from the get-go, is to hide what they did, blame it on someone or something else, or simply claim that the disaster just happened all on its own. Most folks who fix things for a living know what's going on here and just let it all happen, since they know how the story has to end in the long run.

They never condemn or criticize since that's no help, and folks feel bad enough already. Instead we just let them talk, then fix the problem. Maybe we charge a little extra for having to unfix what they fixed so that you can fix what really needed fixing in the first place, and maybe a little bit more for having to listen to all the fibs they told you about what happened.

6   Attibuted to Mark Twain, http://brainyquote.com/quotes/quotes/m/mark-twain109624.html

One day I was in Syracuse, helping just such a person. Nothing was working and, of course, it was all IBM's fault, not his. Having been around the block a bunch of times, I could see where the problem really was: I was looking at him.

You know, it's funny how scripture can reflect real life so accurately. Some folks do prefer the darkness; most likely an ego thing. But scripture also says that the Lord is kind and full of compassion, slow to anger and abounding in love, and that we're supposed to be that way too, so I simply absorbed the anger being hurled at me, didn't accuse anyone of anything, or even try to defend IBM or myself.

Then I suggested that we roll up our sleeves and see what we could do. He agreed condescendingly to let me try. We got past his initial fear and hostility with a mix of compassion and humor. Then we began to mop up and organize the effort to get him back on his feet.

As we went through it I explained to him what things meant and then gently challenged him to explain back to me how he might use the things I was showing him, so I could correct his misunderstandings and build up his self-confidence when he got it right.

Some of the weird stuff that you can only know through years of experience I just did for him myself and let him stand in awe of the mystery. I could sense that he was beginning to see that there was much he had yet to learn.

Over time his tone went from being condescending and aggressive to being grateful and accepting. He could see that things were getting lots better, and I could tell that he was becoming less afraid that he'd be punished or fired.

As we worked together, he began to explain to me how he had mistakenly thought things worked before. I agreed with him that yes, many others had thought it was like that too; it was easy to see how he could have misunderstood, but it wasn't like that at all in real life.

At the end of my time there, when things were looking pretty good, he turned to me and said, "Do you really have to go now?

I wish I could just put you in a jar and keep you here, so I could take you out when I get in trouble."

We laughed, but I knew what he meant. We had wrestled a victory out of the jaws of disaster. We had started that day in angry hostility and ended it in warm friendship. Life was good and he didn't want it to end.

Maybe our egos don't like it when God shows up in our lives to straighten things out, but it's a good thing God does show up. And as we watch the evil unravel and the good appear in its place, life becomes very good in a very special way. We don't want it to end, and indeed, sometimes we get a hint that it really won't.

Hospital Visit

Like many other folks who do similar things, I spend some time each week visiting people at Hartford Hospital. One day last winter I spent some time with a young man, let's call him Jim, who had had some serious abdominal surgery. He had one of those bags attached to him, and it didn't look as if he could move much without pain.

His family was there with him. I knew from my information sheet that they were Catholic, so I greeted them and asked if they were up for a visit. They were indeed, and wasted no time telling me how angry they were at God, indignant at the suffering their innocent son had to endure.

What had Jim done, they wanted to know, to deserve such a thing? Where was God, anyway, and why had he forsaken both them and their son?

"You're one of those religious guys, aren't you?" they asked. "If you have an answer, tell us."

Now those of you who have ever been in a situation like that know that you can't say just *anything*. What would *you* have said? Let me tell you what happened and you can compare it with what you'd have done.

I suggested to them their son hadn't done a thing to "deserve" his suffering, any more than Jesus had "deserved" crucifixion. Life's hard, but it's not like that. God doesn't inflict suffering, nor is God indifferent to it, even though it can sure look like that from time to time.

Then I reached out, touched their shoulders and said gently, "If you want to know what God really thinks of human suffering, turn and look at each other in the face, and look deep. What you'll see is the plain truth of what God thinks about human suffering. God's in the middle of it with us, right here, right now."

As they did that, I invited them to look around and see if they could sense any way in which the presence of God was surrounding their son and the hundreds of other people in the same boat as him in the hospital that day.

Before anyone could say anything, Jim stared at me and said "I can see something. God sent you." I got uncomfortable for a moment because I don't think of myself as being anything special, but before I could get in God's way I found myself saying, "That may be so, Jim, and if it is, it's just part of the story. Your mom and dad, your brother and sisters, everyone who's taking care of you here — they're all part of God's presence too. Let's go even deeper, Jim. You yourself — you're a huge part of God's presence for all of us."

It got quiet and I could tell the wheels were turning. So I prayed some more and this came out: "As you move on in life, Jim, maybe you'll find out about other people who are going through what you're going through right now. You'll be able to encourage them, help them get through their pain, and give them hope, just as all of us are doing for you."

"Sure, you're suffering now — that's just the plain harsh reality of it — it stinks and there's no sense pretending it doesn't. Your blessing and the meaning of what you're going through now will be evident to you later, when you reach out to others who have to go experience what you're going through now. You'll be able to help them in ways the rest of us can only imagine because you've actually lived through what they're living."

"Probably at some point they'll look at you the way you looked at me just now and say, 'Jim — thank God that God sent you to me.' They will have answered their own questions about God and suffering, and they'll know what they have to do next themselves. If there's any story like the one you're writing with your life right now, it's the passion of Jesus."

Then I stopped. It got pretty quiet for just a few seconds, and then Jim's dad looked at me and said, "Thanks. It helps a little to look at it that way." We agreed that it didn't make it any easier to see his son's suffering, but there was hope in the mix now, where there had been little or none before.

Good Friday

There's a Good Friday story about a law professor who teaches at a big Catholic university not all that far away from here that I'd like to share with you. He's a good man — I think you'd like him — but he's a real taskmaster. He says he owes it to everyone to turn out the best lawyers he possibly can, so he demands a lot of them. As it turns out, he's a very devout Catholic and also something of a nut; he likes to do crazy things to wake people up to the goodness of God.

One day he announced to his students that he was going to give them a test whose outcome would determine whether they would pass or fail his course. The test was going to be given on Good Friday. The students complained that Good Friday was supposed to be a day off, but he told them it hadn't been a day off for Jesus, and it wasn't going to be one for them either, so show up or fail. With one of those smiles only professors like that have, he told them the only way they could prepare was to know everything. His students were not amused — how could they know everything?

Good Friday came and the students sullenly came into the classroom. There were assigned seats, spaced at a distance from one another. On each desk was the test itself, and a blue answer book for them to use in which to write their responses.

The test instructions said "You are to follow these instructions to the letter. First, read all of the questions carefully, because you must answer them all. When you have finished reading all of questions, and only then, put your answers in the blue book on your desk."

The questions ranged from interpretation of the code of Hammurabi, eighteenth-century admiralty controversies, and semi-conductor intellectual property law. The students were stunned — this was all just so unfair.

Some were visibly angry, others began to cry, and you could feel the hate well up in that room like the stink in a swamp. A few started to leave the classroom, and the rest just wearily opened their blue books, resigned to the inevitable.

What they saw in the answer books made their jaws drop. Some burst out in laughter, others in tears. Those who were leaving sat down again, puzzled, and opened their own blue books to see what was going on.

On the first page was a note from the professor, addressed to each student by name. This is what it said:

"Every question in the test has already been answered for you. The answers are complete and correct, and you will receive an 'A' for the course."

"You have not merited it, nor is there any way you could have studied for this test in anything short of a lifetime. I have done this for you, exactly this way, because I love you. I owe it to everyone to make you the very best lawyers you can possibly be, and the very best lawyers do not quit and do not despair."

"If you hated me just now, you are forgiven. I've already forgotten it and encourage you to do the same."

"Today, as you know, is Good Friday. Jesus didn't have the day off and neither did you. On this day, Jesus took the test of life for you and me and answered every question perfectly. You and I are redeemed — we receive an 'A' for life."

"We have not merited it, nor is there any way we could have accomplished it ourselves. It has all been done for us simply because we are loved. If you remember nothing else about this course, remember what happened here on Good Friday."[1]

Tulips

What's really and truly ours, anyway? Perhaps it's our attitudes that come closest to being something that's truly ours. Selecting from among the many options our emotions and experiences present to us, we can choose attitudes of love and compassion, patience and gentleness, or the opposite. The choice is ours, and that's what we give to others that's *really* ours, every minute of every day.

Let me tell you two stories about how this works that our fellow parishioners told me recently. Shortly before Easter, one of our delightful young ladies was shopping over at the mall, and decided to buy some yellow tulips for the dinner table. As it turned out, she got the last pot of yellow tulips and happily put it in her cart.

Just then another woman came along, looking for yellow tulips herself. Not seeing any, she asked where our young lady had found hers.

"I didn't see any others," she said. "I think I got the last one."

The other woman sadly remarked that she had hoped to get yellow tulips because they were her child's favorite color, and asked if there was someplace else nearby where she might be able to get some.

Without hesitation, our young lady reached into her cart, took the pot of yellow tulips and gave it to the other woman. Surprised and delighted, she protested at first, but our neighbor told her it was not a problem and the lady simply smiled broadly and said "Thank you!" marveling at how a complete stranger could be generous like that. But that's the way it is among the people in our community. They give away what's really theirs — not so much tulips, but kindness and unselfish generosity — call it love.

I do need to finish the story — it doesn't end just like that. At the exact moment they were exchanging the tulips, the door to the storeroom behind the florist opened and a worker brought in a huge box full of yellow tulips, way more than either one of them could've ever used.

It seems that God is not going to be outdone in either kindness or generosity. Both women happily went off with the tulips they desired, and something else too — a glimpse perhaps, of the way things are in the kingdom of God.

Tommy And His Dad

The storms many of us face in life can severely test our faith. There's a story about little Tommy, and the storm his family faced that I'd like to share.

One day Tommy's dad came home early from work. Tommy ran to greet him at the door with a hug, but his father pushed him away. "Not now, Tommy," his father said, not even looking at him. Tommy was puzzled and hurt — his father had never treated him like that before. Later, he could tell from the tone of his parents' conversation that something was wrong. The tone was dark, the way clouds are in a bad storm.

Later that evening his mom sat down with Tommy and his sister and told them their father had lost his job and was very sad. He wasn't ready to speak with them just yet and needed some alone time.

"Why is Dad sad?" Tommy asked, "He can just get another job, can't he?"

"It's not easy to get a job these days, Tommy," his mom told him. "We need to pray for Dad. He's very upset and disappointed in himself. That's why he pushed you away, Tommy. He feels like he has let us down. He doesn't feel worthy to be my husband or your dad."

Tommy wanted to run and give his dad a hug. Of course he was worthy to be dad – who else could put a worm on a hook? Who chased the bear out of the backyard last summer? Who else really knew how to field a grounder or make a canoe go straight? He was the best dad there could be.

Tommy's mom told him Dad was pretty sad just then, and that it wouldn't be a good idea to try to talk to him. Just the way it was when Tommy skinned a knee, Dad needed time to get over the shock of losing his job and heal a bit. So they prayed instead. It felt good to hear Mom's voice and how confident she was that God would take care of them.

Later, Tommy drew a picture and wrote a note on it to his dad, telling him that he loved him no matter what, and all the ways his dad was the best dad in the whole wide world. He gave it to his mom, and in his little heart he hoped that his dad would read it.

Later that evening, when Tommy was in bed saying his prayers with his mom, his dad came into the room. He had Tommy's note in his hand. Tommy looked up at Dad and could see that he had been crying. Dad sat on the bed and said:

"Thank you for this, Tommy. This is the best note I've ever gotten from anyone. When I lost my job this afternoon I thought I had lost everything. I see now that I haven't lost anything — at least anything that really matters. I have you and your mom and your sister. We all have God. The sting still comes back from time to time, but I think it'll go away before long. Thank you, Tommy. I love you, son."

He looked at his wife and said, "You're right, time to let go of what isn't around anymore; it's time to trust that God will take care of us. I'm not afraid anymore." They gave each other a hug and a kiss and turned out Tommy's light.

It wasn't an easy or short storm in Tommy's family. As winter set in they kept the thermostat low and everyone wore thick sweaters. There were plenty of nights when it was just hotdogs and soup for dinner, but no matter what, they always said grace, asked God to help them, and expressed their love and trust in God and in one another.

It took the better part of a year for Dad to land a new job, but when he did, it turned out to be a good one, and he actually made more than at his last job. He liked the people he was working with, and soon the conversation around the dinner table was full of amazing and funny stories Dad brought home from work.

A month or so later, when Dad's cousin Ted lost his job, Tommy listened with pride in his dad as he phoned and told his cousin to have faith in God, treat his family well, and let his family treat him well.

The best part was when Dad told his cousin to hang on while he got something, ran upstairs, came back with Tommy's letter and read it over the phone to his cousin. Among the many other fabulous things his dad could do, Tommy saw that now his dad could help other people weather their storms, too.

Trip To Hawaii

The chilling reality is that if we shut God out of our lives by making *God* nothing in particular, we've likely shut out everybody else, too, including the real truth about our inmost selves.

Let me tell you a little story that illustrates the point. I was in the hospital a few weeks ago visiting folks, and I met a guy who had recently been to Hawaii, as had my wife and I. He had children who lived there, and he liked to visit them frequently. On one such trip he'd had the good fortune to get an upgrade to first class.

As he was settling into his seat by the window, a guy with a beard sat down in the aisle seat next to him. He was dressed like a middle-aged hippie gone kinda long in the tooth and wide at the equator.

The first thing he did was to turn not to my friend, but to the man across the aisle, who had been staring at him oddly. He smiled and said: "Sure, I'd be happy to give you my autograph." Well, the other guy just looked down his nose and said "I don't need your autograph. Who do you think you are, anyway?" My hospital friend's seatmate just said with a sigh, "Oh, nobody in particular."

My hospital friend thought that the whole exchange had been rude, so after the plane took off, he turned to his seatmate, smiled, tapped him gently on the arm and asked, "I don't mean to be nosey, and you can tell me to mind my own business, but are you someone famous? If you are, *I'd* like to have your autograph, if that's okay." The guy was delighted, turned to my friend with a smile and said: "I'm Meathead."

At first it didn't register with my friend. What kind of person tells people his name is 'Meathead?' Then it hit him like a bombshell — the guy sitting next to him was Rob Reiner who, among many other things, played Meathead in the 1970s sitcom *All in the Family.* They had a long and fascinating conversation and yes, he eventually did get Reiner's autograph.

When the plane landed, the man across the aisle who had snubbed Reiner and then never said anything at all on the seven-hour flight from Dallas to Honolulu, waited until Reiner left the plane, then turned to my friend and said "If I'd known it was Rob Reiner, I would've treated him differently."

My friend said he wondered for a moment what to say to someone who thought like that. Then he just looked at him with a faint, incredulous smile and said as gently as he could "I don't think you would've treated him differently if he had been Jesus Christ." He didn't tell me what happened after that, but you see, my friend knew that what we make of anyone is what we make of everyone.

Mr. Dobson

It seemed to me a while ago that if I really wanted to understand what a particular New Testament passage meant and what scholars were saying about it, it would be helpful to be able to read one or more of the original Greek texts myself.

There are lots of books out there that you can buy to help you learn Greek. Among them is a book by John Dobson, an Englishman who teaches classical literature.

I was wondering which one to get when I noticed that Dobson's book, unlike the others, had a little section in the back addressed to teachers, containing hints for them to help students learn. Curious, I turned to this section and knew immediately that this was the book for me. The first hint to teachers was "Love your students." It was obvious that this was the book for me!

Loving The Right Way

More than one poet has suggested that it's impossible to love someone too much, but that it *is* possible to love them the wrong way. I suspect that many of us, if not all of us who have bumped against life's sharper edges, know exactly what they're talking about.

Indeed, even the gospel illustrates how ancient that insight happens to be. People flocked to Jesus, but for the wrong reasons. They were attracted to Jesus by what he could do for them, not by who he was.

It reminds me of the story about Nancy, who dated a wealthy Wall Street trader a few years ago, just before the economic crisis in 2008. It seemed like a storybook romance. Tony took Nancy to all the fanciest restaurants and showered her with expensive clothes and jewelry. Any girlfriend of Tony's had to look the part.

Nancy enjoyed the gifts and going to parties with the rich and powerful. She was impressed by the respect and deference with which Tony was treated. Her parents and siblings liked the arrangement too, because they got to be included in some pretty fancy doings themselves. As Tony put it, any relative of Nancy's was his relative, too.

The only holdout was Uncle Vinny, who told Nancy that Tony was all sizzle and no steak. "He uses people," Uncle Vinny told Nancy. "You're just arm candy for this clown. He doesn't know who you really are, and Nancy, let me tell you — guys like him don't care about finding out, either."

Nancy thought Uncle Vinny was just being over-protective. Maybe guys had been like that down in Jersey City when Uncle Vinny was growing up, but Tony was different. He loved her. He even said so.

Then the market began to crumble. Nancy noticed that things between her and Tony were changing, too. They weren't invited to as many parties, and when they were, the respect and deference for Tony that had been there before was missing. Some people even seemed angry, but Tony wouldn't talk about it when Nancy asked.

The stream of gifts dried up. Tony seemed increasingly distracted when they were together. Their conversations became perfunctory, and Tony didn't seem interested in her any more. Nancy felt that her world was collapsing.

Maybe Uncle Vinny had been right. Maybe she really had just been Tony's arm candy. Nancy began to doubt that Tony had ever really loved her and wondered that if he had, whether it was just for what she appeared to be rather than for who she really was.

As she pondered what was happening, it occurred to her that the shoe fit on her foot, too. Maybe she had valued Tony for the gifts and prestige, and never really cared to discover who he really was.

It stung a bit when Uncle Vinny suggested that maybe both of them were avoiding the hard work of getting to know each other, and the inevitable awakening to a surprising thing or two about themselves in the process. If they really loved each other at all, they loved each other the wrong way. Not long thereafter, Nancy and Tony broke up.

I don't know where Tony is these days, but Nancy's going out now with a pretty decent guy. If you ask her about the difference between Jeff and Tony, she says "That's easy. Jeff is all about reality, not appearances. It isn't always pretty, but he loves me the right way."

Jesus makes it clear that he wants to gift us with reality: the truth about God's love for us, the truth about his relationship both to us and to our Father. To believe in Jesus is to accept the gift of Jesus himself, and to enter through him into the relationship he himself has with his Father. To believe in Jesus is to love the right way.

Let me tell you another little story. A friend of mine is probably one of the most cheerful volunteers you ever met. He has an infectious laugh, shares himself like an open book, and would probably give you his last dime if you asked for it. When you're around this guy you sense that you're in the presence of some-thing larger than life itself.

One day we were yakking about deep stuff and he told me that for many years the first thing he did in the morning was to thank God for his lovely wife, their fabulous children, their home, food, a job, and all the good things with which they've been bless-ed. As time went on, the children grew up and left home. He was able to retire, but unfortunately his wife developed cancer and died shortly thereafter.

I remarked that that must have been harsh and he agreed, but then continued: "You know, Tim, my life has been full of wonder-ful blessings. As they've changed from what they were to what they are now, my morning prayer has changed too. I used to thank God just for all the good things with which he surrounded me."

"Now I thank him simply for who he is, as he is, in his eternal, sovereign almighty self, and as he lives and works his mysterious will in this chunk of time through little old me."

"I know I've always loved God, but I turned a corner when I woke up one day and understood that my life wasn't just about me. With the focus off me and all the good things God has done for me, I find I want to love him for who he really is rather than just for what he can do for me. I want to love him the right way, and when I fill my heart with the body and blood of Jesus that's what happens."

In that moment I knew what it was that made it seem as if I was in the presence of something larger than life itself when I was around him. I *was* in the presence of something larger than life — something good, something eternal — the presence of God in a person who has both been gifted, and also who has chosen, to love God the right way.

Dogs

One day not too long ago I was visiting folks in the hospital and found myself chatting with one of the patients about pets. He had a couple of dogs and I told him my family had one for many years, too. We laughed together as he'd tell me a story about one of his dogs' odd habits, and I'd come back at him with one about our dog, too.

Every dog is different, I suppose, but ours liked bread. We could go into the kitchen and open any other drawer, and he'd just lie in his spot quietly, until we opened the bread drawer. Then his ears would perk up and he'd leap out of his spot like a rocket, race over and sit there quietly at our feet, with this look of profound hope and expectation on his face.

Sometimes he'd get something and sometimes he wouldn't. When he got a crust or two he'd wolf them down and then sit there with that look of hope and expectation again. I used to wonder in amazement just how much bread he could eat! I don't think we ever discovered his limit.

When he didn't get anything from us, he'd give us this awful look of disappointment. Then he'd walk back slowly to his spot, plop down, and issue a deep sigh. He knew all about bread. It was *so* good, and he couldn't get enough of it.

I was wondering about that, thinking about the wonder of the Eucharist. Jesus, the Bread of Life, is *so* good too, but in ways far beyond what animals like dogs appreciate, and which we can have trouble understanding too.

Unlike any other food I can think of, this food consumes us even as we consume it. It's curious that it works that way, but then again, it's God's intention that your redemption and mine be worked out by his Son becoming one of us. As my friend Fr. Tony says, "To eat the flesh of Jesus and to drink his blood is to become totally identified with his very person, with his deepest thoughts, with his vision of life, with his values, and with his mission to build the kingdom of God."[7]

7   fr.tonykadavil; http://frtonyshomilies.blogspot.com

Even more curious is the way Jesus remains with us in the Eucharist. At some level, the bread and wine not only become the body and blood of Jesus, but they also symbolize the whole dynamic of what's going on. Redemption involves God and humankind together; creator and creation working together.

God makes the grapes and wheat. We make the bread and wine. God sends his Spirit to make these become for us the body and blood of his Son. We step up to receive this and become the way in which God remains vibrantly present in his world, as visible to people as Jesus was in his day. We enter into a fundamental unity of life and purpose that some might call the kingdom of God.

As I pondered this unity, I recalled that my new friend and I had continued to chat about our dogs, and found ourselves talking about the different breeds there were and what they were like.

He told me he'd read somewhere that all the different kinds of domesticated dogs we have today can be traced back to a single pack of wolves living in China about 15,000 years ago. Beneath all the diversity in dogs that we see nowadays lies a deep unity. At some level, the dachshund has much in common with the Saint Bernard, and the gentle golden retriever isn't all that far removed from the sometimes not so gentle pit bull.

So it is with us too, when we view life through the unifying prism of the Eucharist. Beneath all the diversity and things that separate you, me, and all the other people in the world, there's an underlying unity of Eucharistic love that's willed by God. It's not any more visible than the genes that make dogs similar, but it's undeniably there.

The gospel tells us that many people had difficulty at the time with the idea of Jesus giving us his body and blood to eat, and many people have trouble with it nowadays, too. Perhaps the reality of the Eucharist is just not self-evident to them. But so much of the rest of life isn't obvious either, yet it's perfectly true. Let me give you a special example that might help explain how that can be.

There's a capability you and I have called "blindsight," that allows us to see things in near darkness. Have you ever walked around your house in the dark and just *known* the wall was there, or something else was in your way? That's blindsight at work.

It seems that there's a pathway from our eyes to the interior parts of our brain that doesn't pass through the part that's responsible for conscious awareness. So even though we don't consciously know what's there, our body does.

Our faith operates in a similar kind of darkness. Precisely *how* the bread of life is as Jesus says, his body and blood, his presence and his life, doesn't matter anywhere near as much as the fact that it really is. It's similar to how we may think about blindsight: it doesn't matter *how* it was that you didn't slam into the wall in the middle of the night, it's just a good thing you didn't.

We're all pretty amazing creatures, loved by God in ways we cannot even begin to imagine, but in ways that God does not wish to withhold from us simply because of the limitations of human understanding. God wishes to fill you and me with his love, transform us, and join us to himself.

Imagine yourself at church now, and let your soul be filled with hope and expectation. Imagine that God's in the kitchen and moving toward the bread drawer. Imagine yourself receiving the Eucharist: not just a simple crust to enjoy in the moment, but the Bread of Life, the life of God himself, to enjoy without limit, forever.

The Best Of Neighbors

Roy and Ed were neighbors, friendly enough with one another, but with quite different temperaments. Roy was a calm, peaceful sort who just took life as it came. His wife, Pam, and their kids were like that, too.

Pam and Roy encouraged their children as they grew up to pray and then follow their hearts. They coached them to focus on one interest at a time and then give it everything they had.

Although they exposed their children to many possibilities and were happy to share their opinions when asked, Roy and his wife were careful not to bully their children. No expectations or demands about particular careers or interests were ever expressed.

The kids themselves would need to do the hard work they had to do to discover their true identity and the mission that God had for them, not to become just who their parents thought they ought to be.

Ed was different. I suppose we'd call him a type-A, hard-driving sort. He had worked hard and developed a large and successful retail business over the years. Ed knew what he wanted life to be like, not only for himself, but also for his customers, suppliers, the world in general and his children in particular.

He had decided that his eldest son, Larry, was going to take over his business as he got older. The only problem was that Larry had no interest in his father's business. He sensed that his mission in life was to work with disabled children: that was who he was. This angered and frustrated Ed. He belittled his son's dreams and threatened to cut him off if he didn't come around.

One day Ed was over at Roy's. As they were talking, Ed angrily mentioned his disappointment with Larry. Roy listened quietly. Then he invited Ed to come help him with a little carpentry project he had going in his garage.

Ed was up for that, and they went into Roy's garage together. Handing Ed a wrench, Roy asked him to take a couple of screws out of a bracket holding up a shelf. Ed laughed and said. "How am I supposed to take screws out with a wrench?"

Roy just laughed back and said, "C'mon Ed, a tool's a tool, just do the job."

"Don't be stupid, Roy. It's the wrong tool," Ed said, "What kind of idiot would try to take screws out with a wrench?"

"Yeah, I guess you're right, Ed," Roy said. "Maybe it's like the way Larry's the wrong tool to run your business."

Ed was shocked. He glowered at Roy and said, "I know how to run my business."

Roy stared back at Ed and said, "Larry doesn't. Wrong tool, Ed. The man you want him to be doesn't exist."

Ed put the wrench down, turned around without another word and walked back home. Roy watched him go and wondered if he had said the right thing.

He got his answer a few days later. After dinner, the doorbell rang. Roy opened the door, but nobody was there. A small box with his name on it lay on the top step. He took it inside and opened it together with his wife and children.

Inside they found a screwdriver and a wrench, and a little note that said, "Thanks, Roy." It was signed by Ed and Larry, with a note that simply said "You know a lot more about tools than we do, Roy. Don't lose these — we may need to come over and borrow them again, or maybe some other tool — you never know."

Divorce

Jesus declared that God's intention before the fall was that men and women were to be equals in their relationships, deeply committed to each other in exclusive bonds of love. Their relationships were to mirror the kind of relationship that God had with Israel.

The Hebrew Bible is full of covenantal language that speaks of God's relationship with us as if it were a marriage. In such a relationship there's security, not uncertainty; respect, not privilege; responsibility, not entitlement.

The deep truth is that all of the relationships into which we are drawn are invitations to mirror in this world the equality and love that exists between the Father, the Son, and the Holy Spirit. For Jesus to have said anything other than what he did, especially about marriage, would've required him to tell us something that simply isn't true about the interior life of God.

Life is hard, however, especially in a fallen world, and one of the most difficult parts of all is any human relationship. It can be hard to know what our responsibilities are, especially when some of those relationships fail. Let me tell you a little story about that.

A few years ago a good friend of mine, let's call him Ernie, learned that his brother was divorcing his wife. The news had deeply troubled him. That evening after dinner he told his wife and children, and they too were shocked. As the news sank in, they began to talk.

"Why are Uncle Bob and Aunt Alice getting divorced?" Ernie's teenagers Roger and Tina wanted to know.

"Uncle Bob says they haven't gotten along for a while now, and they just can't stand to be around each other anymore," Ernie said. "I don't get it — they seemed like the perfect couple to me."

"I'm not so sure about that," said Ernie's wife, Sally.

"How do Pammy and Wendy feel? What will happen to our cousins?" Tina asked.

"Pam and Wendy are very sad and confused," Ernie said, "They don't like it. Sometimes they think they caused it, but Uncle Bob and Aunt Alice have told them it isn't their fault, and that's a good thing — kids are never the reason parents get divorced."

"I'm worried for them though," Ernie said. "I suppose Pammy and Wendy will spend equal time with each parent after the divorce. I hope they'll do okay, but the odds aren't in favor of things being as easy for them as they'll be for you and Roger, Tina. They'll need all the compassion, prayers, and help they can get. It's especially important for us to let them know we still love them the same as ever."

"What about Bob and Alice?" Sally asked.

"I don't know," Ernie said. "I told them to keep on coming to church with us. They'll need God's help to get through. You know, divorce isn't just a legal and financial thing. There's a spiritual, intellectual, and emotional part to separation too. For some people, it feels like a slow death. Everyone, including us, has to go through the grieving process."

"We aren't personally involved in their divorce, Dad," Tina objected.

"Oh yes we are," Ernie said. "Divorce affects more than just divorcing couples themselves. Take a look in your heart — isn't there sadness there?"

"Well, yeah," Tina admitted.

"Same for me and Mom and Roger too, I'll bet, and that's actually a good thing, Tina," Ernie told her,

"The sadness means we love them. We share their brokenness and grieve over what's happening. God doesn't ask us to judge either of them — just the opposite. Our relationship with each other and with God is better than that — God simply asks us to love them, as-is. It's so important that they be able to find love, peace, and acceptance when they're with us. It can give them hope and help us all to heal."

Everyone nodded. Then the children looked deeply into the eyes of their mom and dad and asked, "You and Mom are doing all right, aren't you?"

Sally and Ernie were taken aback at first, but then they realized what their children wanted to know. Reaching out and drawing them into a big family hug, Sally said, "Yes, we're doing just fine."

Ernie looked at his wife with affection and said, "I'm for Mom and Mom's for me and we're for you and God's in the middle. I pray to God and give thanks for that every day."

It got quiet as they all huddled together in their circle of love. Then Tina looked at the rest of her family through tear-filled eyes as their hug untangled and said, "Thanks, everyone — that was perfect."

Computer Wisdom

Not all that long ago, a customer of mine called in a panic and told me his computer had stopped working; it wouldn't even turn on. I told him to relax and do exactly what I was going to tell him to do. He promised that he would.

After checking the obvious, I told him to unplug the computer, remove the case and then gently but confidently wiggle every little integrated circuit (those little black chips you see inside) and every connector he could find; then plug the machine back in and try turning it on again.

He called back in about an hour. In an awed tone he said, "The thing came right back on. How did you know to *do* that?"

I chuckled, because I know I'm no magician. Anyone who works with these things has found out either from personal experience or having someone tell them, that vibration, corrosion and such like can cause a large percentage (up to 70%) of these kinds of problems. This is just one of the first things you'd try when a machine suddenly doesn't work anymore. I told my customer it was simply wisdom, passed on from one generation to the next, like our faith.

So it is with God's wisdom. We don't have to understand it all the time, maybe not even most of the time. Sometimes all we have to do is do what we're told and trust.

Oh, and by the way, if your hard drive fails, try putting the machine into the freezer for about an hour and then restarting it again. Trust me.

Learning From The Pros

I was talking with a friend of mine the other day who isn't Catholic and he complained that we Catholics worship the saints.

"We don't worship the saints, Jim," I told him. "We simply ask them to intercede for us with God. As we pray, we also remember how the saints met the challenges in their lives which we ask for help in our own lives."

"I go directly to God," Jim said. "I don't need any saint to help me."

I thought about that for a moment and then said, "Hey Jim — you and I play golf, right?"

"Sure," he said. "What's that got to do with being a saint?"

"Are you a good golfer?" I asked.

"No, and you aren't either," he reminded me.

"Right," I agreed. "Now if you wanted to get as good as you could get at golf, to whom would you go for lessons — me or Jack Nicklaus?"

"No offense, Tim," Jim said, "but I think I'd choose Jack."

"Well, it's the same thing with the saints," I told him. "You'd go to Jack instead of me because he has demonstrated his abilities and he has the titles to prove it. Same with us and the saints: we go to them because they're the winners; they have the titles. We want them to show us how to do what needs doing in our situation, just the way we'd like to ask Jack to show us how to putt."

"You mentioned that you pray directly to God, Jim, but I wonder, do you think you'd attempt the pro circuit without ever taking a lesson?"

Jim mumbled something and didn't agree outright, but I could see that he got the point. That's the way it is with the saints. Their lives serve as lessons for us — why not learn from the pros?

Hospice

A few months ago I was visiting a man in the hospice unit at Hartford Hospital. He was due to be discharged later that day, to go home to die. He was not all that much older than me, thin, sharp-featured, bald, and alert.

I explained who I was, and he decided he wanted to talk. As we began to chat, he became animated, and made his way out of his bed to a chair next to mine. As we began, it quickly became clear that he wasn't interested in small talk.

He began to tell me about his life — things of which he was proud and things he wished he'd never done; people he had loved and others he had hated; opportunities he'd embraced, and others he had let slip through his fingers.

He wasn't Catholic, and wasn't looking for confession or conversion. He simply needed a reasonably compassionate, non-judgmental human being to listen to him express what his life had meant, to be present as he reflected with gratitude on the gifts and talents with which he had been blessed, and to let him acknowledge his errors, failures, and shortcomings.

Some of what he said he spoke with thoughtful gravity, other parts were humorous, and some was spoken with the nervous resignation of a student who realizes a bit too late that he hasn't studied enough for his final exam. He looked at me, and asked me what I thought God would make of him.

I told him I wasn't in charge of the universe and simply trusted in God's mercy as much as he could too, if he wished: God knows what God has made. I suggested we just take a look at two passages from the Bible – the prodigal son and Psalm 103. He had heard about the prodigal son and understood the message, but he wasn't familiar with Psalm 103 and wanted me to read it to him. I did. It goes like this:

Bless the LORD, my soul; do not forget all the gifts of God,
Who pardons all your sins, heals all your ills,
Delivers your life from the pit, surrounds you with love and compassion,
Fills your days with good things; your youth is renewed like the eagle's.

The LORD does righteous deeds, brings justice to all the oppressed.
His ways were revealed to Moses, mighty deeds to the people of Israel.

Merciful and gracious is the LORD, slow to anger, abounding in kindness.
God does not always rebuke, nurses no lasting anger,
Has not dealt with us as our sins merit, nor requited us as our deeds deserve.

As the heavens tower over the earth, so God's love towers over the faithful.
As far as the east is from the west, so far have our sins been removed from us.
As a father has compassion on his children, so the LORD has compassion on the faithful.
For he knows how we are formed, remembers that we are dust.
Our days are like the grass; like flowers of the field we blossom.
The wind sweeps over us and we are gone; our place knows us no more.
But the LORD'S kindness is forever, toward the faithful from age to age.[8]

He liked that psalm. I asked him if he thought he was in a spot where he could place his faith in a God who treats his creatures like that. He said he wasn't sure. I gently suggested to him that many of the problems some people have with God are actually problems they have with themselves — disappointment that they have not measured up to some perfectionist's notion of who they think they ought to be.

God is far less harsh a judge than many of us can be, especially with ourselves. If judgment is about anything at all, it's about truth in the heart, not about performance. As Mother Teresa reminded her nuns, and all of us too, God calls us to be faithful, not successful. I could see the wheels turning in his mind.

I wanted to continue to tell him that in taking off our own egos and putting on Christ, as Saint Paul urges us to do, our perspective on our own destiny and the vastness of God's mercy changes

8   Psalm 103

both dramatically and irreversibly, but I never did. It appeared from his expression that he had said what he needed to say and heard what he needed to hear. No further talk was necessary. Certainly no more theology. So we sat there together in comfortable silence for a while. Just two of God's creatures, present to one another; one going home to eat a tuna sandwich and write a homily; the other going home to die.

A little smile came over his face, and he seemed more at peace than when we'd first met. Then he turned to me, nodded his head and said "Thank you. You've given me hope." I nodded back and said, "Thank *you* — it has been a fabulous privilege to share these moments with you."

Indeed it had been. I know where the hope he sensed had really come from, and I knew who the author of those privileged moments had been. The sense of the presence of God at that moment was so palpable that I felt we both could've reached out and touched him. The room was alive with light and love; that room was vibrating with hope.

I pray that each of you may experience a blessing like that. May you experience the blessing of those few graced moments when the love of God envelops and penetrates everyone and everything so thoroughly that there seems to be nothing else in the room.

The time will come soon enough for all of us when it'll be someone else who's going home to a tuna sandwich while we're on our way home to die. Whether someone's there to chat with us or not, may we anchor our hope at that time, if we can, in our faith in the compassionate God who made us and redeemed us, who knows us inside out and loves us unconditionally.

Get Out Of Jail Free

Let me share the story of Alice, Timmy, and their family with you. A few months ago, as has happened to so many folks here, their dad, let's call him Ted, was told by his boss that the only way they could keep him on and pay his benefits was if he could accept a 40% pay cut.

That came as a thunderbolt. Sure it was good just to have a job in times like these, and to have the benefits, but there was no way they were going to be able to pay the mortgage and eat with a 40% pay cut. In a flash, the anticipation, the joy of Advent and Christmas evaporated. To Ted, it seemed just then that God was going away, not coming.

He went home sad that evening. His family knew that something was wrong, but Ted couldn't find the words to tell them what had happened. He felt like a failure and he was depressed. For several days it went on like this. His wife, Nan, and little Alice and Timmy were sad, too.

They wondered if it had been something they had done. Ted didn't say. As often happens in situations like this, they began to wonder if there was something wrong with who they were. Ted didn't say.

"What's wrong with Dad?" Alice asked Mom one day after school.

"Yeah, Dad seems so unhappy," Timmy added. "Why won't he talk with us anymore?"

"I don't know," Mom said. "He just seems so depressed. Let's pray for Dad."

And they did. As they prayed, Alice said, "Maybe he just can't find the words to tell us."

Mom winced as she thought about all the different things that could be behind Ted's sudden, unexplained reluctance to talk.

"I have an idea," Timmy said. "Let's give him a 'Get Out of Jail Free' card from the Monopoly set. You can write a note, Mom, and tell him what it means."

"Maybe we can find a Bible passage, too," Alice said. "Dad likes God."

Everyone's mood brightened a bit, and they sprang into action. Mom got a pad and some envelopes, Timmy found the "Get Out of Jail Free Card," and Alice hauled the family Bible over to the kitchen table.

They worked together busily for an hour or so, cleared off the kitchen table and left a set of numbered envelopes for their Dad to open. They decided to hide — Dad would have to choose to open the envelopes on his own, and he'd probably need some time alone to figure out what to do next. Mom told them what the signal would be to come out of hiding.

Ted came home to a darkened house, turned on the light, and saw the envelopes on the kitchen table. He wasn't sure he wanted to open any of them. But he did, starting with envelope #1.

In it was the "Get Out of Jail Free" card and a note from Nan. All it said was "We love you, Ted. Whenever you're ready, please use this card and come back to us. If there's anything to forgive, consider it forgiven. If it's anything we've done, please forgive us. Something's got you in jail. We love you, and we want to see you set free. Please open the other envelopes, too."

Ted sank into a chair at the table. He was overwhelmed. His family had given him permission to do what he hadn't been able to give himself permission to do; to do what he didn't think he'd ever be able to do, and to say what he never thought he could've said. A tear formed in his eye as he opened the second envelope and read the note inside, clearly in Timmy's handwriting.

"Dad," it said. "You like God. We found this in the Bible. It's from the Proverbs part. 'Every day is miserable for the depressed — the happy man has a continual feast.' (Proverbs 15).

Love,

Timmy and Alice and Mom"

Through his tears Ted let out a little chuckle. "Kids," he thought. "They can see right through you." As he was thinking that, he looked up. The lights had come on in the other room. Everyone had heard the signal – a chuckle from Dad.

Nan and the kids came to the kitchen door. "Is it okay to come in now?" Nan asked.

"Depends," Ted said. "Only if I can use this card." He held up the "Get Out of Jail Free" card and wiped his eyes.

His family ran into the room and gave him a giant hug. It was messy and noisy in that kitchen for a while, as you might imagine. Ted told everyone what had happened, and they each reflected to each other what it had been like for those terrible few days.

"We'll get through this, Ted," Nan told him. "Far worse things could've happened. Let's work through it together, as a family."

"We love you no matter what, Dad," Alice and Timmy said, giving their Dad another big hug.

Ted said to them, "I feel as if this huge weight has been taken off my back. I couldn't bear the thought of having let you down, and I didn't know how to talk about it. It was like I was wandering on some tortuous winding road that led nowhere. Everywhere I turned, all I could see was another obstacle. Now I truly feel as if I've been liberated from prison. Whose idea was that 'Get Out of Jail Free' card, anyway?"

His family laughed and told him to open the third envelope. It was a letter, neatly typed and signed:

Dear Ted,

"Every valley shall be filled
and every mountain and hill shall be made low.
The winding roads shall be made straight,
and the rough ways made smooth,
and all flesh shall see the salvation of God."

Your family prayed and let me fill in the valley of the depression you were in. They prayed and let me flatten those mountains and hills for you. They prayed and let me straighten out your path for you.

Welcome back home again, Ted. This day I've come to you and once again you're within the circle of love. We actually never left — you did — in sad, self-imposed exile. In your liberation from that you've gotten a glimpse of what it means to 'see the salvation of God.' If you happen to think of it when we're together in prayer some time, maybe you can help me flatten some other people's mountains too. Stay in touch.
Your friend,
God

Ted grinned at his family and asked, "Did God really write this?" Nan and the children just laughed and looked back at him with love and joy. In that moment, exactly that way, the newly liberated Ted got his answer.

Chapel Miracle

Let me tell you a story one of our fellow parishioners told me just a few weeks ago. It seems that there was a man among us suffering terribly from what a CAT scan suggested was a particularly aggressive form of cancer. Things did not look good.

One evening, the man's wife went to visit him in the hospital. For some reason, she couldn't see him immediately. She asked if there was a chapel in the hospital where she could pray, but was told no, there was no chapel. So she waited elsewhere.

Her husband went home with her to rest and await a biopsy operation later that week that would tell them what the monster in his midsection really was. By this time he had lost 35 pounds.

That evening, the man's wife prayed at her husband's side, invoking the assistance of Saint Jude — the patron saint of desperate cases — to help her as she called out to Jesus for a cure. Then she touched her husband's body where the evil was.

Her husband leaped up from bed and rushed to the shower — he felt as if he was on fire. He angrily asked his wife if she had poured hot water on him. But in a minute or two he calmed down — he realized he had been cured of whatever it was that had made him so sick.

His doctor didn't believe him. Nobody got that better from being that sick that fast. So a few days later, he went into the operating room and the surgeons opened him up to take the biopsy. They couldn't do it — nothing was there any more. They checked everything, to make sure they weren't trying to remove tumors from a guy who just wanted his tonsils out. But no, they had the right person, and the CAT scans were as good as CAT scans get. The chief physician said that in forty years of practice he had never seen anything like it.

Just as in the gospel story of the ten lepers who were freed of leprosy, our fellow parishioner was freed from whatever had stricken him. So what did they do next: go to Disney World like the nine ungrateful lepers? No, just like the tenth leper, they prayed with praise and gratitude to God. Not only that, the woman remembered that there had been no chapel for her to pray in at the hospital. There is now. She and her husband saw to it that it got built, with plenty of help from their friends in our parish and elsewhere. That is a pretty decent expression of thanksgiving, wouldn't you say?

Dave And The Football

Dave used to like to play touch football with his friends after school when he was younger. One day when they were playing, a group of older kids they didn't know came along and started making fun of them.

Dave and his buddies ignored them at first, but then the older kids came onto the field and grabbed Dave's football. They tossed it back and forth among themselves, laughing at Dave and his friends and pushing them away roughly as they tried to get their ball back. Eventually, they just ran off, taking the football with them.

Dave and his friends went home sad and angry and told their parents what had happened. Everyone was upset. The police were called, but offered no consolation since no one knew who the older kids were. Somehow the peaceful fabric of the neighborhood had been torn apart by the injustice of the bullies who had stolen Dave's ball. People wondered if things could ever be the same again in the neighborhood.

A week or so later Dave was in the supermarket with his mom. As he was going down the aisle someone tapped him from behind. It was one of the kids who had stolen his football, dressed in a supermarket apron. From under his apron he took out the football and held it out to Dave.

"Here's your ball," he said to Dave. "Sorry we took it."

Dave didn't know what to say.

"After I got home I felt bad," the young man continued. "Something inside told me I was wrong. I wanted to give you your ball back, but I didn't know where you lived. So I brought it here and hoped I'd run into you or one of your friends. I'm really sorry, man. Here."

Dave felt angry, but something inside told him to stay cool. Things were being set aright, and he could tell that anger would ruin it, so he simply reached out and took the ball.

"It won't happen again," the young man said. "Promise."

Their eyes met, and in a moment, anger, shame, forgiveness, and understanding all flowed together in a silent stream between the two of them. Dave nodded, touched the young man's arm and watched as he turned and walked away.

Dave and his friends still talk about what happened. They agree that in some sense things never were the same again in the neighborhood after that. No, things had gone from bad to good in a way that taught them all something about the reality of evil and the possibility of redemption.

Gifts of the Magi

There's a story about a young dad whose birthday happens to be on the Feast of the Epiphany, and it contains a clue about what you and I can give to a God who has everything.

Our young man and his wife had three little children, Alice, Tommy, and May, all well under ten years of age. Since they were little they didn't have much money, but they still knew all about gifts. They knew that gifts were good to give and to get, and that it could be as much fun watching someone open a gift as it was to receive gifts themselves. They also knew you could say something with a gift that sometimes could be hard to say in words.

So they asked their mom what they should do. Well, their mom was no different than the moms here, so she told them, "You are the best gifts Dad has ever gotten." But they still wanted to give him something, so she said, "Go make something special with your own hands. Dad would like that better than anything you could buy at a store."

So off they went, and when Dad came home that night they gave him their gifts. Dad was a good person, just like you, so he made a big deal out of it. Alice was the youngest, so her gift got opened first.

It was a picture of a golden retriever. Dad gave her a big hug and asked what the dog's name was.

"King," little Alice said.

"Why did you give me a picture of a dog named King?" Dad asked.

"Because you're like a king, and you're like a dog, too," Alice said.

"Tell me more," Dad encouraged her.

"You're like a king because you take care of us and make the rules," Alice said. "And you're like a dog because we can hug you and you play with us and you're never mean and we feel safe when you're around."

Dad thought that was pretty good, and so did the rest of the family.

May's turn came next. Dad opened the gift and inside was a small bag of cinnamon cookies.

"Man, do these smell good, May!" Dad exclaimed, passing the cookies around to his family. "How did you decide to give me a bag of cookies?"

"Cookies are good and so are you," May said. "I like the way they smell. I like the way you smell when you pick me up and hold me. I feel happy."

Everyone thought that was pretty good too, and munched on the cookies.

Tommy's turn came next and Dad opened his gift. It was a big rock with his name painted on it. "Wow Tommy, a rock!" Dad said. "Why did you decide to give me a rock?"

"Because it's big and solid, like you. You can use it to hold the shed door open when you're working in the garden. And then when you're dead we can put it next to Grandpa's in the cemetery and bury you under it. You won't have to buy a new one that you never get to see."

Mom was appalled but Dad thought that was pretty original.

Each of the children's gifts were like the gifts of the magi in some sense. They revealed something about what their dad meant to them. His gentle response said much about how he loved them. The children were able to say things with their gifts that aren't easy to say sometimes in ordinary conversation, just like the story of the Magi's gifts let authors of the gospel say complex things about Jesus.

Do It Your Way

A friend of mine, John, passed away last November. He and his son-in-law, Phil, were quite a pair of entrepreneurs. They set up and ran several businesses large and small around here over the years, and the world's a better place for their having done so.

Phil told me they didn't always see eye-to-eye. Sometimes they'd talk over an idea and get excited about it, but then disagree about a point or two. Then each of them would get convinced he was right and the other was wrong and they'd start hollering at each other. At some point John would just stop, fold his arms, and simply tell Phil, "Look — do whatever you want."

Phil would stop too, and check.

"You mean that?" and John would say, "Yeah."

Phil would probe again, "I can do whatever I want?"

John would say, "Yeah, have a ball."

Then, with a smile on his face, Phil would march off in triumph to his doom.

Invariably he'd fall flat on his face without John.

Then Phil would come back to John and try to explain.

John would just sit there quietly.

Then Phil would say that maybe he should've tried harder.

John would stay silent.

Then Phil would wonder aloud whether others had deliberately tripped him up. Still, not a peep would come out of John.

Finally Phil would understand the silence and say, "That was a pretty stupid idea, wasn't it? We should have done it your way."

Then John would say, "Hey look, I've been working on this great new idea! What do you think? Let's do it together!"

Now, that always astonished Phil. If he had been John, he used to say, there would have been a death in the family — his. It didn't seem to matter how much time or money had been lost, or how much pain John must obviously have gone through watching Phil do something he knew was doomed to failure.

One day Phil asked me about that. I shrugged and ventured a guess: "I think your father-in-law loved you, Phil. Maybe more than he could tell you, or you could hear." I remember him thanking me for putting into words what he'd often felt but couldn't express. What John did was so much like the way God treats us. No guilt, no blame, no humiliation or dwelling on the past. But no progress either until Phil first came to his senses and acknowledged the truth.

Halloween

Last week, on Halloween, we enjoyed all the children who came to our door in their costumes. One little girl showed up dressed in a pillow case with a couple of holes cut out for her eyes and mouth. We asked her what she was and she said, "A girl."

We laughed and asked her, "OK, that's what you really are, but what are you dressed up as?" Then she told us she was a marshmallow or something, I forget.

Seems like little people don't have much trouble being clear about who they really are and what they're only pretending to be. Maybe that's why God is so fond of them.

Older folks can have problems doing that sometimes. Jesus rebuked the religious leaders of his time for observing the letter of the law, but not the spirit, and for oppressing the very people they ought to have been serving. Somehow they had lost touch with who they really were and what they were called to be.

We heard last week that the greatest commandments of the law were to love God with everything we've got, and to love our neighbors as ourselves. We celebrate the gift and the challenge of this law in the rituals of our sacraments.

But if the mere outward form of the rituals ever becomes for anyone a substitute for actually loving God and neighbor, and showing it in what we say and do in daily life, we have lost touch with what we have been called to be and are engaged in a dangerous form of self-deception.

In the gospels we see Jesus urging people to recognize the emptiness of mere religious formality, and the abuse of self-importance disguised as leadership. It has never been easy to do that with leaders. Indeed, the confrontation had the most serious consequences for both Jesus and those to whom he spoke.

You might have heard about Bishop Oscar Romero. He was a bishop in El Salvador back in the '70s. That was a period of terrible repression in El Salvador. Fourteen families controlled 40% of the land, and death squads roamed the countryside, killing with impunity anyone who opposed them. The powerful people in El Salvador approved of Bishop Romero's appointment as Archbishop, because he was seen as an orthodox, pious bookworm who had never spoken out publicly about anything. He would not be dangerous to them.

The day after his election, a priest, an old man, and a seven-year old boy were murdered by death squads. It was a priest Romero knew well — he was the first priest he'd ever ordained. He had been a simple priest, a quiet yet persistent advocate for the poor in his parish, and inconvenient to those in power.

When Romero drove out to pay his respects to the victims he looked deeply into the eyes of the poor parishioners who had also come to honor their priest. They stared at Romero. He saw in their eyes the gaze of Jesus, a gaze that simply asked, "Are you bringing us hope, or not?"

It was the pivotal point of Romero's life. He had been a good priest and bishop to his people, but this time he was being asked by God through his people to choose between taking the gospel seriously or taking another path: to know yet ignore the redemptive truth burning in his heart, and to spend the rest of his life complicit in his own peoples' oppression, simply pretending to be their devout religious leader.

He made his choice to be an authentic disciple of Christ. No masks. No pretending to be someone he knew he could no longer be. The military hated him. The power elite feared him. The US Government ignored his pleas to cease military aid. He was finally shot to death while saying mass, two days after the biggest political rally in the history of El Salvador, when he had pleaded with the soldiers in an army at war with its own people, to stop the repression. This world's judgment on those who confront its evils is repression and death, yet to fail to do so is to die as men and women before our bodies die.

Perhaps we are not called to such heroic destinies as Bishop Romero. Whether we were called or not, and whether we respond or not, is between each of us and our God. The gospel invites you and me to approach that pivotal point of stark honesty in our lives; to look in the mirror together with Jesus and ask: Are we like the old Romero — pious and orthodox, but careful not to offend? Or are there injustices that we need to confront in our own lives, in our own web of circumstance and relationships? Are we in touch with what God's law of love calls us to be, or are there masks that we need to drop?

At our particular judgment, right upon death, the complete and unmasked truth about who we really are will confront the infinite, loving truth that is God. On that day, it will be perfectly clear to us and to our Creator just exactly who we were and who, perhaps, we were only pretending to be.

Who Are You?

There's a story told about an executive who was stuck at the airport a few years ago. His flight had been cancelled because of bad weather, and he was at the end of a long line of passengers waiting to be re-ticketed on other flights. Becoming impatient, he elbowed his way to the front of the line and roared at the ticket agent that he had to get home and get home now. When she told him that everyone else in the line had the same problem, he exploded and screamed at her, "Do you know who I am?"

The agent gave him an interesting look, picked up the microphone and announced on the terminal loudspeakers: "Your attention, please. There is a man at gate 26B who does not know who he is. If anyone can help this person, please come to the gate now. Thank you."

Now the rest of that story cannot be repeated in a sacred space, but you can be assured that the ticket agent, as well as everyone in the line made it abundantly clear to that executive just exactly who he was and who he wasn't.

The gospels tell us of John the Baptist, who was a man quite unlike that executive. John was perfectly clear about who he was and who he was not. Since he was pretty popular, John certainly had the opportunity to make a big deal about himself, but he didn't. He knew himself well and chose to be who he really was; He was the one who was to point to the hidden action of God in Jesus that was about to unfold.

To the bewilderment of the religious executives of the time, he simply didn't fit neatly into any category with which they were familiar. He was not who they expected him to be — they had never seen a herald of the Lord.

Like John the Baptist, we are called to be heralds of the Lord too. It's a fundamental part of who we are and what we're doing here. Pondering our own identities as heralds, acknowledging the truth about our sinfulness the way John led people to do, we can grow more and more aware of our urgent need for redemption and enter deeply into the Advent spirit of anticipation.

In our thoughts and prayers about who we are and what we're doing here, we too can sense the hidden action of God through Jesus in us that transforms this world day by day into the kingdom of God, to the extent that we let it be done unto us according to his word.

What answer would you give if Jesus approached you and asked you who you were? Somehow I doubt that any of us would reply with just our job title or Social Security number. Perhaps we'd sense that he was really looking for something more from us — a clarity about ourselves that John the Baptist had.

One way we can move our minds to develop that kind of Advent clarity is to put ourselves directly into the gospel, by name. As I reread the gospel stories about John the Baptist, I sometimes put my name in, just to enter into the story more deeply. Perhaps you can do that yourself sometime, putting your own name in and change the "him's" to "her's" as necessary. Listen to what that sounds like:

A man named Tim was sent from God.
He came for testimony, to testify to the light,
so that all might believe through him.
He was not the light,
but came to testify to the light.

And this is the testimony of Tim.
When the Jews from Jerusalem sent priests and Levites to him
to ask him, "Who are you?"
He admitted and did not deny it,
but admitted, "I am not the Christ."

So they asked him,
"What are you then? Are you Elijah?"
And he said, "I am not."
"Are you the Prophet?"
He answered, "No."
So they said to him,

"Who are you, so we can give an answer to those who sent us?
What do you have to say for yourself?"
He said:
"I am the voice of one crying out in the desert,
make straight the way of the Lord,
as Isaiah the prophet said."

It sounds pretty real, doesn't it? A conversation like that could happen over in the mall and nobody would think twice about it.

When we do an exercise like this, what do we learn about who really we are? Each and every one of us has been sent by God, on a mission.

What are we doing here? We're heralds, like John, testifying to the light, the truth about God, in everything we say and do. In everything we choose not to say and not to do. And we are asked by God to do this so that all may believe.

Are we someone special? Not in the sense that the world usually means it, like our selfish executive back at the airport. Were we to do that, it would only show that we don't really know who we are.

When we're true to being the heralds of the Lord that we really are, then the Lord's way is made straight. For you and me to be heralds means that because of what we say and do, it becomes easy and natural for people to believe in him. They see that we are comfortable with our redeemed humanness, and take delight in the Lord who takes delight in revealing himself to us through each other.

What do people see when they see us? Are we what they expect, or are we part of the quiet but powerful Advent shockwave that announces the in-breaking of the kingdom of God?

It's so important to see our own true selves, to be clear about who we are and who we are not. For it isn't until we know and accept who we really are that we can answer from the depth of our true selves the question Jesus will pose to Peter, and to all of us just a little later on: " Who do you — the real you — say I am?"

Gina And The Leaves

Once upon a time, a little girl named Gina decided she wanted to know when the end of the world was going to be and what it was going to be like. She asked her dad, who was out raking leaves. Dads, of course, know everything.

"Dad," Gina asked, "when is the end of the world going to be and what's it going to be like?"

Dad looked at her with love, smiled and said, "Personally, I think it'll be on a Tuesday, but I don't know which one. And it won't be all that bad, I think, if we're prepared."

"Why on Tuesday?" Gina wanted to know.

"Because Tuesday's about the most ordinary day you can think of, and no one would be expecting it to happen then," Dad explained.

"You're making that up!" Gina said.

"Yep, I am" Dad said. "So is anyone else you'd ask to tell you about the end of the world. All we know is that it'll definitely happen to each of us when we die, and maybe to all of us together if the end of time really does come next Tuesday. We just have to be prepared."

"How do you prepare?" Gina wanted to know.

Dad sat down with her together in the leaf pile, and brushed his hand through the leaves.

"These leaves know how," he said. "Maybe they can tell us."

"What do you mean?" Gina asked.

"Well," Dad explained, picking up a leaf, "the leaves came into being from the tree, just like we come into being from God. Then they do what leaves are supposed to do: make food for the tree, give birds a place to hide their nests, make oxygen for us to breathe. Some need to give themselves up as food for insects and animals. All of them are so beautiful to look at, even after they've fallen from the tree, aren't they, Gina?"

Gina agreed that leaves were pretty neat. "But how do they tell us how to prepare, Dad?"

"Well, Gina," Dad said, "every leaf accepts the truth about itself, knows how it's expected to serve, and every leaf does so without complaint. When the time comes for it to die, it accepts that too, for the leaves know that it's through death, down through the earth and into the roots that they will come to be part of the tree again, in the way the tree needs them to be next. Every leaf in my little pile knows that and has embraced the full meaning of its life. You don't see any of them hanging up on the tree any more, do you?"

Gina looked up and indeed, the tree didn't have a single leaf left on it.

"No, I don't," Gina said. "Do you think leaves get angry or afraid when they see they have to fall?

"I'm not a leaf, so I don't know," Dad said. "All leaves eventually fall anyway, so it probably wouldn't be helpful to be angry or afraid. That might get in the way of doing what leaves are supposed to do."

"Every living thing, if it can think about it at all, has to be grateful for the privilege of being alive, even if sad things happen to it from time to time. Somewhere in the gift of life lies the capability to love and forgive, to trust and let go. Somewhere in the gift of life lies the grace of God, close enough for all of us to touch, in ourselves and in one another."

Then they sat there together quietly for awhile in the cool autumn air, breathing in the rich smells of the leaves and the earth, watching the sun sink behind the trees.

"What do you think the leaves teach us, Gina?" Dad asked.

"Do what you're made to do," Gina said, giving Dad a hug. "I think I was made to love."

Dad smiled, and as the darkness deepened, he gently picked her up and carried her back into the warm light of their home.

Investments

The folks who were on US Air flight 1549 found out something about how to invest their time well. One of the passengers interviewed right after his rescue said that as the plane was going down into the Hudson River everyone just started to pray.

He sounded a little sheepish about that for some reason, but those of us who have been there know that being that close to death can really focus a person's attention on what's important. Somehow, all of a sudden, the right investment becomes brilliantly apparent.

That's harder to do in ordinary life, when one day follows the next in such a predictable way that it seems as if this life is all there is. Even ordinary life is full of sudden surprises. When I visit people at the hospital, I often find it's the people visiting the patients more than the patients themselves who need to talk.

I had a conversation with a young lady last week who was visiting her boyfriend. His sudden, totally unexpected illness had turned their lives upside down.

"Everything changed, just like that," she told me. Their time had run out, and they hadn't even heard the clock ticking.

I agreed and told her that many of the really important changes in our lives are sudden. I told her retirement was like that too — one moment you're working, the next you're retired. Bingo. The only thing you can hope for is that you've invested well and planned for that retirement. You're ready or you're not.

She agreed, but wondered how a person could know when the best time to start to plan was. I suggested to her that immediately was probably the best time. She nodded and laughed and went off to get herself a cup of coffee.

As I moved on to the next room, I wondered about that — maybe that was why the disciples dropped everything and followed Jesus immediately. What, after all, was there to think about, especially if you've awakened to the fact that you've already got the payoff in hand and he's actually right there in front of you?

So it is with the investment choices for our own lives. We need to plan for our retirement from this world. No way of knowing when it'll occur. Might be a good time to check our portfolios — maybe see where we're placing our trust these days. Immediately is probably a good time to start, and trust me, there's no more secure investment in this world or the next than the love of God in Jesus Christ!

Patty And The Blind

One day young Patty went to her dad with a problem. There had been an argument in the lunchroom at school. One of her classmates was a fundamentalist in his religious tradition, and decided he needed to tell everyone who didn't believe what he believed the way he believed it that they were going to hell.

"I started to tell him I was a Catholic but he didn't even let me finish my sentence," Patty said. "I was definitely going to hell because we pray to Mary instead of God, call mere men 'Father' and listen to the pope instead of just the Bible."

"What did you and your friends do, Patty?" her Dad asked.

"We just let him go on, Dad," Patty said. "I wanted to tell him we pray *with* Mary, not *to* her and are just being respectful and honoring our tradition and all that, but nobody could get a word in edgewise. He only wanted to see things his way."

"What a shame," Dad said. "If he's that kind of blind he'll never get to know you, or maybe even anyone, more than superficially. I wonder if he'll ever really get to know God."

"He could spout Bible passages from memory," Patty said, "He sounds like he knows God pretty well."

"Perhaps he does," Dad said. "But I wonder how close that relationship really is. Knowing *about* God isn't the same thing as knowing God. If he won't listen to you to find out who you are, why would anyone think he's listening to God? You're an expression of God's love just like everyone else, but it seems he doesn't want to see that. Sounds like he thinks he knows it all. "Did I ever tell you the story about Mr. O'Toole before he got married?"

"No," Patty said.

"Before he married Mrs. O'Toole he had gone out with a woman who worked for the CIA."

"Wow — I didn't know that," Patty said. "How come they didn't get married?"

"O'Toole couldn't stand it, Patty," her dad said. "Every time they went on a date she would tell him everything he'd done since their last date."

"That's creepy, Dad," Patty exclaimed.

"Your friend at school is like that, too," Dad continued. "Imagine yourself at a party where someone walks up to you without introducing himself and starts telling you who you are, without ever asking you anything about yourself."

"That would be weird, Dad," Patty said.

"And suppose when you tried to correct him, he angrily told you that you were wrong about yourself and told you to shut up."

"I'd call you, grab my coat and run, Dad," Patty said. "Nobody really does that, do they?"

"It's done all the time with God, Patty," Dad said. "Folks who've never introduced themselves to God start telling God what God's all about, and prefer their own stories so much they decide that not only God, but the rest of us need to know too. Sometimes I think the worst form of blindness is to be only able to see things the way you happen to think they are."

"Are you saying my friend at school is like that, Dad?" Patty asked.

"I can't say — I don't know him," Dad admitted. "To know people you have to listen to them, it seems to me, and listen deeply. Before I ventured an opinion about your friend at school I'd want to invite him to introduce himself to me — sort of the way we invite God to introduce himself to us when we pray intentionally."

"I've never invited God to introduce himself to me, Dad," Patty said. "People have just told me about God."

"That'll carry you for a while, Patty," Dad said, "But to grow up and to see God in more and more of God's lovely splendor, you have to issue that invitation, get some practice in being really quiet and attentive, and let God introduce himself in your life in the way God sees fit. I think you'll be pleasantly surprised, if not downright astonished, at how that introduction goes. God won't show up uninvited, and I'm sure you don't want to stay in the dark about God."

It's All Unconditional

As I was chatting with a bride and groom-to-be, I told them about a couple I'd met visiting folks at the hospital. Let me tell you, too.

They were a couple in their early nineties, comfortable with their spirituality, and in very good shape. I told them I was a deacon, and they seemed pleased to hear that. We jabbered for quite a while, and they told me they'd been married for 66 years. My jaw dropped and I said they'd been married longer than I'd been alive! They laughed and looked at each other with love. I asked if they'd tell me about it.

It was a classic love story, a Navy man and high school sweetheart, but the part that struck me was that they both said they'd always been best friends. I asked how they thought people came to be each other's best friend, and they used the phrase I had used with my young bride and groom-to-be: "It's unconditional commitment, Tim. It's the only way that happens."

I nodded and invited them to tell me about that. "We were so in love," John, the husband, said. "We tried for years to have children, but apparently that was not to be for us. Cindy thought I would want a divorce, but I told her my commitment to her was unconditional.

Then one day we were talking and almost at the same time we said to each other 'We're all God's adopted children — why don't we do what God did with all of us and adopt a child?' And so we did. We came to find out that having a child meant unconditional commitment too."

"When we started looking into it," Cindy said, "we thought we'd be adopting a baby, but the agency we went to said that there were many older children waiting for adoption too. We asked about that and the woman with whom we were speaking became very intense."

She told us: "Their birth parents were unable to provide for them. Their foster parents couldn't give them the permanent family they needed. Caseworkers have moved them from home to home, causing painful changes each time. These children feel they've been let down by every adult they've encountered. They need at least one adult who makes an unconditional commitment to them. They need that commitment before anything constructive can happen."[9]

"We asked what she meant by 'unconditional commitment.' She explained: 'Unconditional commitment' that there is nothing a teenager can do to stop being someone's child. They long for that kind of love. Do you think you could do that?"

"John and I weren't sure we could, but the lady we were working with told us that patience, understanding, kindness, and empathy, along with unconditional commitment to the child, would get us past the hard parts."

"I remember telling her that it sounded like basic Christianity to me," John said, "and she looked me right in the eye and said: 'That's exactly what it is'."

"So we ended up adopting our Anna," Cindy said. "At first it was hard — she tested us to see if that unconditional commitment was real. Once she learned that it was, something beautiful happened. You see, Tim, the response to our unconditional commitment was her unconditional love."

"We've found that it was like that in our marriage, all our close relationships with people we love, and with God. There's something redemptive about unconditional commitment and unconditional love. Maybe you can give a homily about that sometime."

I smiled and assured them I'd think about it.

9   http://www.adoptinfo-il.org/teensneeduncond/

Perfect Little Annie

Little Annie was her parents' only child. They all loved each other very much and Annie's parents always told her that they thought she was the perfect little princess.

One day the perfect little princess was in the kitchen and smelled something wonderful. Her mom had just made a batch of chocolate chip cookies and there they were, in the middle of the kitchen table.

"Can I have one?" Annie asked.

"No, Annie," her mom said, "I've made them for the old people over at the convalescent home. Please don't take any."

"Okay," Annie said.

Now, I'm going to guess you know how this story proceeds. Sure enough, the smell of those cookies was too much for little Annie, and when she saw that the kitchen was empty, off she crept, up to the cookie pile, and snagged one. There were so many, she thought, her Mom wouldn't miss just one.

A short time later her mom came up to her and asked:

"Annie, did you take one of my chocolate chip cookies?"

Annie turned red and said, "No."

She was perfect little Annie, after all, and perfect people don't do things like that, do they? And even if they do, they wouldn't want others to think that they did.

"That's funny," her mom said, "I made thirty cookies and now there are only twenty-nine. Someone at the convalescent home is going to have to go without a chocolate chip cookie and just sit there watching everyone else enjoying theirs. Are you sure you didn't take one?"

Poor little Annie felt awful. She told her mom "No" again and crept off to her room to hide.

A few hours later her Dad came home from work, walked by her room and noticed that Annie was crying. He went in and asked her what was wrong.

"Nothing," Annie said.

"Do you think people who say they're crying over nothing are telling people the truth?" her Dad asked.

"I am telling the truth," Annie protested.

"Maybe you're telling me what you'd like the truth to be," her Dad said, "but you're probably not telling the truth to yourself. When you feel up to it later on, why don't you come down stairs and tell me or Mom. Maybe we can help." Then he left Annie alone.

Sure enough, in a few minutes Annie came down and found her mom and dad sitting at the kitchen table. She walked up to them slowly, feeling more terrible with each step.

"I took a cookie," she said, her head hanging down. Like the rest of us, Annie felt awful. It's like that every time we have to face a hard, unpleasant truth that contrasts starkly with the images we have about ourselves.

"We know," her parents said. "We were wondering when you'd decide to tell us."

"You knew?" Annie asked.

"Sure," her parents said. "Who else could've taken it?"

"I'm sorry," Annie said, and started to cry. "Am I going to be punished?"

"Deciding to come downstairs and tell us the truth was punishment enough," her Dad said, giving her a kiss. "Why don't you have a chocolate chip cookie instead? Mom made two batches, you know. The second batch was just for you!"

Annie didn't know whether to laugh with delight or continue to cry, just for effect.

She took a cookie and asked her parents "Am I still perfect?"

"Now you are," her parents said. "A perfect person isn't someone who never makes a mistake and never does anything selfish. Nope. A perfect person is simply someone who doesn't hide behind a mask like a child on Halloween does.

Perfect people, holy people, see and accept the whole truth about themselves, including what they do that's wrong from time to time. Since they're really holy, they're willing to do whatever it takes to make things right again with other people and with God as soon as they can. That's what makes them perfect."

The $20 Web

There was a teacher in a Catholic high school not too far from here who wanted to awaken his seniors to something important before they graduated.

One day he took out a $20 bill and put it on a desk in front of them. Then he said "This goes to the first person who can tell me exactly what it is." Everyone's hand went up, except for a couple of guys and gals who just kinda sat there and smiled.

The first person he picked said "That's a $20 bill."

"True, but that's not exactly what it is," the teacher told him.

The next person said "That's a Series S $20 Federal Reserve note."

"That's also true," the teacher said. "But it's still not exactly what it is."

The third person said "That's a piece of special cloth with special ink printed by the US Mint in the form of a $20 bill that we can use to buy stuff."

"Or maybe earn...or save...or invest...," some others suggested. The teacher could tell from the looks in their eyes that they were beginning to get it. There was more to this $20 bill than met the eye.

Then he called on one of the kids who had just been sitting there smiling. "What do you think?" he asked.

"That's a piece of cloth that came from a factory that was run by a whole bunch of people who used ink made by a whole bunch of other people in another factory somewhere..." one of them started to say.

"Yeah, who all woke up one morning and had breakfast made by some farmers who grew stuff and raised animals..." another smiley sort said.

At this point everyone started to laugh because they could see where the discussion was going. The teacher asked "How long do you think it would take us to describe what this $20 bill really and exactly is?"

"Forever!" they all said, laughing out loud. They were beginning to get a sense of the vast web of relationships that the mere existence of the $20 bill implied.

"That's right," the teacher agreed. "Please remember that when you go off on your own in just a few more months. Think of every point in your life as if you're standing at the top of a huge mountain whose base is hidden in the mist, every atom of which is connected to every other."

"You can't see it all, yet if it all isn't all there, you wouldn't be standing at the top of anything. At every single moment, you're enmeshed in a vast web of relationships with everyone who has ever gone before you, stretching out behind you in time, just as you will be part of the web of relationships for generations untold who will come after you."

"These are the folks who grew your food, invented and built your automobiles, airplanes, and everything that works in your house, defended the country, made its laws, and ran its marketplaces, your mom and dad and everyone who has ever worked, whether they were aware of it or not, to make it possible for you to have the life you have. And never forget the folks who struggled to keep people aware of the love of God in the middle of it all."

"There are no self-made people, and no one has ever existed who hasn't been in relationship with everyone else before and after him or her."

Then the teacher asked, "Whose mountain is that anyway — the one on which we stand?"

The kids got quiet, but they knew what he meant.

"God's?" one of them asked.

"Right," he said. "And those relationships? At their best — what are they about?"

"Love?" one gal asked.

"Communion?" another suggested.

"You're both so very right," the teacher said, deeply impressed by his kids. "Let me read you a story."

Since it was a Catholic school, the teacher was able to read the gospel story about the foolish man who built a barn for himself and decided to kick back and live the rest of his life as if it were all about him. He knew the kids would understand now what it really meant.

When he finished, he asked, "What do you think this man's biggest problem is?"

"He only loves himself," one person said.

"He doesn't understand that web thing you talked about," another said. "Yeah, he's not in communion – he doesn't see where he fits in," a smiley sort said.

"That's exactly right," the teacher said. "He doesn't see where he fits in with his neighbors and he doesn't see where he fits in with God. I'm asking you to pray with every $20 bill you ever handle. To remember that just as the bill fits into the economy of our nation, you personally fit in to the economy of salvation, and the divine economy of God himself."

God's Song

The folks down at Baylor University do a study every couple of years about religious attitudes in America. In the last study the authors said that our attitudes toward God could be described like this:

- **Authoritarian (28%):** God is angry at sinners and wouldn't hesitate to throw a disaster or two at them.
- **Critical (16%):** God is judgmental, but isn't really going to bother to do anything about it one way or the other.
- **Distant (24.4%):** God is a cosmic force that launched the world and now lets it run on its own.
- **Benevolent (23%):** God sets standards but is inclined to be compassionate towards us.[10]

It turns out that the majority of Catholics and Jews reported that they believed in the distant God.

Perhaps attitudes toward God like these might benefit from some adjustment. Scripture tells us that far from feeling we need be intimidated by an authoritarian, critical or distant God, the truth is that we can actually walk right up to God anywhere, any time and ask for anything. In his very existence, let alone what he says and does, Jesus shows us that God is utterly accessible, and wants to be close to us.

As I thought about all this, I wondered if maybe it's not God who's inaccessible, authoritarian, critical, or distant. Perhaps it's someone else.

Let me tell you a little story that might explain what I mean. Many years ago I worked at the phone company down in New Haven, and had an opportunity to take a short course on internal consulting. It was quite interesting and I learned a lot about myself and other people, much of it pretty surprising.

One of the things they did was to videotape us interviewing a potential client. Video recorders were new back then. It was the

---

10 http://richardsprague.blogspot.com/2006/09/american-attitudes-to-ward-god.html

first time I'd ever seen myself like that and man, was it a shock. The trainer and I watched as I slouched in my chair, stroked my beard sagely, glared at him, and loftily intoned questions using words nobody could understand. I remember thinking "Who does this guy think he is? Wait a minute — that's me!"

The trainer told me the obvious — I didn't look particularly accessible. Just the opposite. I looked critical, authoritarian, and judgmental. No one in his right mind would saunter up to me and ask for help with a project.

The trainer asked me what I was hiding from — what I was afraid of — but I didn't tell him. So he just shrugged and told me that I had to change and become accessible if I wanted to be a successful.

Afterward, I was left to ponder why my outside was so different from my inside, and how that had come to be. It didn't take too long for me to see that this wasn't a phenomenon that only occurred at work.

As I paid more attention, prayed about it, and went through some of the painful changes that had to happen, I came to see that God cannot have a relationship with someone who doesn't exist. The living God is delighted however, to have a relationship with the real you and me; folks who don't really want to hide behind authoritarian, critical or distant impersonations at all — who're really quite the opposite.

To have a relationship with God we need to make ourselves accessible to God, and to allow others access to him through us. The story of my training experience and that study of religious attitudes in America suggests that something might be standing in the way.

There are some hints about what it might be in what Pope Benedict has written about God's accessibility in his book, *Jesus of Nazareth*. Here's how the pope puts it:

> "[God] puts himself within reach....He enters into relationship with us and enables us to be in relationship with him. Yet this means in some sense he hands himself over to our human world. He has made himself accessible and, therefore, vulnerable as well. He

assumes the risk of relationship [and indeed] of communion, with us."[11]

There's the problem with being accessible. Being accessible requires vulnerability. And as with most things that require us to be vulnerable, we accept the invitation reluctantly. No one wants to be judged; no one wishes to be criticized; no one wishes to be rejected or hurt; and everyone wants to be loved. Vulnerability opens us up to all that, but it's risky. Who is seriously going to run that risk and open himself or herself up to anyone, human or God, who's authoritarian, critical, or distant?

If we have attitudes about God like that, then our challenge is to change. By praying as Jesus teaches us, we become aware that the vulnerability and accessibility that God invites us to doesn't involve judgment, criticism, rejection or hurt at all. God's kind of vulnerable accessibility involves only honesty, goodness and truth. We need no defense and need fear no exposure because everything that happens occurs in the spirit of love.

Let me tell you a little story that illustrates what this looks like in real life. My daughter is a musician: she plays the euphonium. She'll tell you that it takes years of practice, determination, and training to turn a talent into a profession.

But something more is required, and it's critical.

Her teacher surprised her one day by telling her that no one cared to hear her play her instrument. "Anybody can be a technically competent musician," he told her. "But what people really want to hear you say through your instrument is that you love them. They don't want a 'perfect' distant professional. They want *you* — up close, vulnerable, and accessible. Close to them. And you will know from their response just how close *they've* come to you too, and how well you've convinced them of your love."

Like my daughter's euphonium, all of creation is God's instrument. Your life and mine are our instruments. Each day God tells us that he loves us, in the ordinary realities of everything he has created. That is the song our Father wishes to sing with you and me in the ordinary realities of our everyday lives.

11   Benedict XVI, Jesus of Nazareth, pp.143-144

It takes the practice of prayer, determination to seek God, and training in God's ways to be able to sing that song along with God. A song that's not authoritarian, critical or distant, and far more than blandly benevolent. It's the song of love sung intensely and up close, by a vulnerable and accessible God with and through his vulnerable and accessible children: you and me.

Soon And Never

Our house probably wasn't too different from yours as our kids were growing up. Everyone had their assigned chores to do and did them well enough.

From time to time my wife or I would ask one of our children to do some special job that was out of the ordinary. And of course, being great kids, they always said "Yes."

But sometimes we'd come by an hour or so later, and it was perfectly clear that the job hadn't even been started. When we looked around, we'd find the child who'd been asked to do it reading a book or watching TV, and we'd inquire if they remembered what we'd asked them to do. "Of course," they'd reply. Then we'd ask "When were you planning on getting started?" The response would invariably be: "Soon."

Another hour or so later we'd find that the job still hadn't begun, so we'd ask again when we could expect them to do it. Once again the answer was "Soon." Now I'm a patient guy, but there's a limit of endurance beyond which my behavior goes non-linear.

As that point was being approached, we'd start to discuss what "soon" really meant. Not surprisingly there was a difference of opinion. In my understanding, "soon" means so close to "now" that you can barely tell them apart. In the kids' view, "soon" meant "never."

Scripture tells us about other folks who thought they would be all right just telling God that they'd be following him "soon." But that doesn't seem to be what God wants to hear from us, does it? Each of us has been asked to do a special job, something out of the ordinary, something unique in the history of the world that for some reason only we can do, and we need to get on with it. Not "soon," but "now."

If you recall, there's a part of the gospel where Jesus asks someone to follow him and the person replies, "Sure, but let me bury my father first." Another way of saying: "Soon."

I read a commentary that pointed out something I hadn't noticed before. The passage doesn't say that the person's father was dead yet.[12] I went back and reread it and sure enough, it doesn't say that. If the person's father was still alive and healthy, then for all we know, he was really telling Jesus he had no intention of following him anywhere, ever.

Jesus' reply sounds harsh, doesn't it, when he says that the dead should bury their dead. It's not only harsh — it's impossible, isn't it? The dead can't do anything anymore. Jesus' message to those who would follow him "soon" is that they're exactly like dead people. Just as mortal life is over for the dead, so spiritual life is over for those whose definition of "soon" really means "never." We don't have to wait for our bodies to die.

So where is Jesus going, that's so important and why is it so crucial that we follow him? The gospel text says Jerusalem, but that's merely his physical destination. Pope Benedict just finished writing a book entitled *"Jesus of Nazareth,"* in which he relates his own journey to find and connect with Jesus.

The pope suggests that the real destination of Jesus is at one and the same time the depth of his Father's being and the depth of yours and mine, on a mission to connect them together in a healing bond of faith, hope and love through the working of the Holy Spirit. It's a trip to the foundations of reality and it's one which we should be taking "now," not "soon."

Have you ever missed out on something really important because your "soon" turned into a "never?" Many years ago I had to go down to New York for an important business meeting with a potential customer. My plan was to drive down to New Haven and take the train.

I got up in what I thought was enough time and sat down to breakfast and opened the paper. My wife watched me, told me I wasn't giving myself enough time and asked me more than once when I was planning to leave.

12 http://desperatepreacher.com/bodyii.htm, Date: 26 Jun 2001 Time: 15:33:59 JRW in OH

I told her "soon" a couple of times, but the paper was interesting that morning and I wanted to finish it. Life was going to unfold the way I wanted it to.

When I looked at my watch I saw that I had exactly enough time to make the express that would get me to New York on schedule, and off I went. It turned out my "soon" wasn't soon enough. Traffic was backed up on Route 4 in the traditional spots and I-91 was a nightmare.

I heard on the radio that a truck had flipped over and I realized that my "soon" had turned into a "never." I knew I was going to miss that meeting. This was in the days before cellphones, too, and I had no way to get in touch with anyone.

As the saying goes, you only get one chance to make a good first impression. Without even having met the people I was supposed to have met, I was already behind the eight-ball.

I was angry with myself for not having left lots earlier — why did I think that newspaper was so important? How could I not know to give myself lots of time? I should've listened to my wife. In the end, was it that I just didn't understand what was at stake, or was it simply that I felt it was more important to do things my way? The reality began to loom in my mind that I was going to lose those new customers, and so indeed it was.

When "soon" becomes "never" by design or neglect in our relationship with God, more can fall by the wayside than a potential customer or a job that needs to get done. What can fall by the wayside is us. We can miss taking that journey to Jerusalem together with Jesus. A journey that is really a plunge in faith into the dark, interior reality of the mystery of existence and redemption. A journey on which we come to realize our true selves and achieve our destiny as children of God.

Take that trip to Jerusalem with Jesus. Promise yourself to do that not "soon," but "now." Let's spend some time as Pope Benedict has, asking God to teach us more about Jesus and his mission.

That will happen, seemingly on its own, as we pray and read, and simply choose to live our everyday lives increasingly in the presence of God. A presence before which we will all eventually be called to stand and give an account of ourselves.

When might that happen? Well, soon. Perhaps sooner than you or I expect.

Trinity

The famous theologian, Karl Rahner, wrote a book about the Trinity in which he remarked that it seemed to him that most folks could get by just fine without it. What he meant, of course, was that the language we use about the Trinity is so complex, and the reality itself is so far beyond what we can conceive of as humans, that it's easy to give up on it very quickly and focus instead on Jesus or some other tangible dimension of our religious belief.

He had a point there, I think. Discussions of the Trinity don't show up much in everyday conversation for most of us.

Experience of the Trinity does though, and I think our experience of Trinity can fill in where the meaning of the words of theologians might go beyond us. Let me tell you a little story that shows what I mean.

I love being a dad, and I always have. When our first daughter, Katie, was born I couldn't get enough of her. With my wife I fed her, changed her, played with her, and sang songs to her, waiting patiently for the day when she would begin to walk, talk, and begin to reveal who she was. That, of course, takes a while and I had to be content with just watching.

One day my wife was out and I was taking care of little Katie. I took her into the family room, rolled out her blanket, and gently laid her tummy-down on the floor. Then I laid down beside her and just watched and listened as she gurgled and flailed around happily on her blanket.

Time went on and a shadow from the family room window began to move across the floor toward her. Eventually it got close enough to get her attention and she stopped her gurgling and flailing to reach out and grasp for the shadow.

As I watched her I chuckled to myself that she just didn't understand. Of course you can't pick up a shadow with your fingers — it's just not that kind of thing.

It's like that with God and us thinking about the Trinity as well. Surely, you and I can't grasp the Trinity with our minds: it's just not that kind of thing. Sure it's there, right in front of us, and in so many different ways, too. Father, Son and Holy Spirit; God, me and you; each of us, the world, and other people. All reflections of Trinity, perfectly real relationships whose full meaning remains unfathomable.

The Trinity forms the deepest pattern of existence, but like the mystery of existence, it shares the attribute that it can be endlessly explored, but never fully defined. And, as my lovely little Katie found out so early on, even though it's really there and you can experience it, you just can't grasp it.

Later on we introduced Katie to the mystery of Jell-o®, too. I will never forget watching her taking a mouthful, knowing she had something solid in her mouth and starting to chew. Then came that amazing "Wait a minute — where did it go!?" expression on her face as she tried to figure out where the Jell-o® went.

Of course, you and I know that it simply dissolved in her mouth. She was just too little and inexperienced in the ways of Jell-o® to realize what was going on. It's like that with us and the Trinity in some sense too. We're just too young, spiritually speaking, to get it.

In eternity, it will be as evident to us as Jell-o® is to us now. In the meantime, we have to live with the mystery as it reveals itself and try as best we can not only to understand something of the Trinity, but to live in loving relationship with other people and our triune God.

Scripture provides us with some insight into how we might go about that. If you recall, Wisdom is described as playing before God, and taking delight in humankind. Want to become wise and learn a thing or two about the interior nature of the life of God? Go play. Play in the sight of God. Take delight in your humanity and luxuriate in the stunning collection of gifts and powers that God has showered upon us all.

Chances are your play will turn on your creativity, and if that isn't among the principal things we share with God, nothing is. When our creativity is turned on it's just a matter of time before we realize that creating stuff is not particularly interesting unless we share it with someone else who can delight in it with us.

You can try it out today, if you want. Go home and make a root beer float — not for yourself, but for someone you love. If you're living by yourself these days make one for someone else who likes stuff like that.

Do it consciously, for the love of the other person and for the love of God, with the intention of delighting both God and the person you love. As you make your float you will most likely find yourself drawn into the same delight that you wish for God and the person you love, and you are then getting an inkling of what the interior life of the Trinity is all about.

Simply enjoy living that playful experience, present to the delightful reality of yourself, God and the one you love. Let the feelings, thoughts, and prayers flow naturally. Don't try to analyze or understand it. You won't be able to grasp it, because it's just not that kind of thing any more than the Trinity is.

If you happen to be on the receiving end of a root beer float today, make sure you say "Thank you." Not just "Thanks," but *"Thank you!"* with enough expression to show that you're as grateful for the wonderful person who made the float for us, and the God who created him or her, as you are for the float itself. That too will provide a glimpse of what goes on within the Trinity, and we will touch what makes up the foundation of the unity among people the theologians speak of.

This is serious stuff, I need to tell you. If someone says playing like this is a goofy waste of time, I'd wonder if that person thinks prayer is too. In both activities we create, form, and communicate our love. In playful prayer and prayerful play, we touch our astonishing destiny.

Flashpoint

The Holy Spirit doesn't just do things on the big screen. The Spirit operates within anyone open to God's whisperings: folks like you and me. Folks like Jimmy and his sister Patsy too — let me tell you their story.

Jimmy was seven when his sister Patsy was born with Down syndrome. That term didn't mean much to seven-year-old Jimmy. All he knew was that he had a new baby sister, but he could also sense that his parents were sad for some reason.

There were other emotions too, that Jimmy couldn't name, but they seemed to be causing his parents deep pain. His mom and dad told him tearfully that Patsy was a special person and would need extra love and care, and that he'd understand more as time went on.

Reflecting his parents' emotions, Jimmy was scared and upset too, and he asked his mom and dad what he was supposed to do. In an inspired moment they told him through their tears just to be open to the Holy Spirit, and to let the Spirit be his guide, just as they prayed intensely that the Holy Spirit would be that for them too.

Prayers like that do not go unanswered. Breaking through the mix of extreme emotions they felt, something surged up from deep within Jimmy and his family over time, and they began to see that Patsy was an expression of God's love just as much as they were.

But then came the flash. One evening at dinner time, as Jimmy tells it, he and his mom and dad found themselves all looking at Patsy together and suddenly being gripped by a vivid sense of some kind of deep, unbreakable bond of totally accepting love that embraced the four of them, and which seemed to extend upward and outward into infinity. In the same moment they all together felt an almost physical jolt of the same kind of supernatural courage that propelled the disciples out of hiding at Pentecost.

For a moment they were confused and even a little bit frightened as they began to talk and realized they were all experiencing the same thing.

"Wait a minute," Jimmy recalled his dad saying, "We're doing this whole thing all wrong."

Indeed they had been. Beforehand, their feelings of embarrassment, shame, and even guilt had been hobbling them and they had wanted to hide both Patsy and themselves. But in a flash, something profound, a Pentecost event, had occurred at that dinner table. Afterward, Patsy was taken everywhere. From deep within came the courage and wisdom to respond to Patsy and those who encountered her, with compassion and strength.

Jimmy watched people's reactions: some were kind, others rude, some were simply uncomprehending. Jimmy saw that part of what the Spirit was leading him and his mom and dad to do was to help others understand and accept Patsy, to broaden their sense of what it means to love.

Somehow doing this was an essential part of helping Patsy have life to the full. Jimmy saw that those they helped like that experienced their own versions of "before" and "after," moving from fear and prejudice to acceptance and love.

Jimmy's grown now, and he works for a Down syndrome support organization not far from here. He hasn't forgotten his Pentecost event, and he has a profound devotion to the Holy Spirit that he brings quietly to his work. His specialty is helping people with the transformation from the "before" of despair to the "after" of courageous, loving acceptance. He's good at it because he knows how it happens.

There's a "before" and "after" in every encounter with the Holy Spirit. It connects the time before Jesus' resurrection to the time after. It connects the "before" time of your life and mine now here on earth with the "after" time of our own resurrection that's unfolding as we speak. In a deeper sense it reflects the "before" and "after" of our transformation into God's children, and in its deepest sense, it's about the meaning of life itself.

Lucky

One of our friends called the other day and told me to be on the lookout for his dog that had gotten loose. If you've seen it, please let him know.

It's pretty easy to recognize because it's blind in one eye, its left ear's been bitten off, part of its tail is gone, its fur is kinda falling out in patches for some reason — but it's safe to touch, they think — it only has three legs because her husband ran over it with the lawn mower, it has no front teeth from bumping into things all the time, it whimpers a lot because it thinks no one loves it and oh, yeah — it smells pretty badly of skunk because — well you know. It answers to the name — "Lucky."[13]

That's just a story of course; please don't go out looking for a real animal like that. But the story does tie in with Luke's version of the beatitudes in a way. To the extent that we associate being blessed with being fortunate or lucky, the people Jesus mentions don't seem to be particularly well-blessed at all — they seem more like Lucky the dog.

What's so great about being poor, anyway? Or hungry, mourning, or being persecuted, for that matter. When something's blessed, we usually think of something pleasant happening. But sometimes being blessed means something quite different, lucky perhaps in an entirely different way.

A friend of mine lost his job a few years ago and went through a terrible time wondering how he was going to feed his family and make ends meet. In the end, he got a far better job than the one he'd had before and today he'd tell you that losing his original job had been a blessing in disguise.

Somehow he and his family know something about each other now, and about God, that they hadn't before. They had come to encounter denial and anger, fear and despair. Wrestling with it all together with their love for each other stretched to the limit,

13 Adapted form a joke of Fr. John Power CP, Holy Family Monastery, ca. 1990

they'd discovered acceptance and forgiveness, trust and hope. It hadn't been pretty sometimes, and it was never easy. But looking back, they say now that they could see the hand of God in it all.

Today Gene says that although he wouldn't wish that experience on an enemy, he and his family nonetheless learned some priceless lessons they might not have been able to have learned any other way. "I guess we're just lucky," he says sometimes.

I smile and nod. Maybe though, it's really that they've been blessed. Jesus himself tells us that there's something about being poor, hungry, mourning or persecuted for his sake that's a blessing in disguise.

It's been like that in Gene's family. Their roots run alot deeper now and connect with God in the way that those of all who place all their trust in God do. Having reached out to God and survived their suffering, they fear it no more. There's a kind of spiritual maturity in that family these days that wasn't there before.

Other people who've share their stories of suffering say very similar kinds of things. Some who have gone through divorce, for instance, are now actively working to help others. Going through it, they may have felt like Lucky the dog, but having gone through the storm and reached the other shore, they know there's a wisdom they have to share now, a blessing they can pass on to others who need it. By the grace of God they've been able to turn suffering into sacrament — a sign of God's presence among us that everyone can see.

Folks like these live the deeper meaning of blessing. They know that something blessed is something that has been set aside or consecrated to the service of God. In their case, they also know that the something that's been set aside is them.

And unlike Matthew's gospel, in Luke the beatitudes are delivered by Jesus not from a lofty mountaintop but on a level field. The point of this is so that we can see that Jesus is down among us, at our level, right there with you and me, going through that suffering together with us.

It has always been that way. Last week we celebrated the memory of a saint who could tell us a thing or two about that.

When we recalled the only native-born Sudanese saint, Josephine Bakhita.[14]

She was kidnapped by slave traders from the fields right next to her home at age nine. Her last memory of her father was to see him cry out in the agony only a parent who has lost a child can know, because he couldn't overtake the kidnappers and rescue his daughter.

She would fall asleep in chains at the end of each day on her way to the slave markets of Khartoum, and awake hoping to find that it was all just a dream, but it wasn't. After being traded and savagely mistreated for years, she was eventually purchased by an Italian diplomat and taken to Italy.

In Italy she gained her freedom and converted to Catholicism when she recognized in Jesus the God she had always felt in her heart since she was a little child but, had never known by name.

She came to love both Italy and the Italian people, and she spent the rest of her life in service to both. She suffered greatly from the memory of her enslavement, calling out in the middle of the night for someone to loosen her chains. But she treated everyone she met with gentle compassion, a smile, and tender care, especially the children, perhaps as she wished she had been treated during her slavery.

Even as she lived her life, and as she suffered a long, painful descent to death with grace and faith, people knew they were in the presence of a saint. In 1978, Pope John Paul II beatified Josephine Bakhita, a woman who knew poverty, hunger, mourning and persecution first hand, the first saint of Sudan. If that isn't a blessing, nothing is.

Perhaps if any of us are suffering, and feeling more like Lucky the dog than one of God's favorite children, we can ask Saint Josephine to pray *for* us and *with* us, to help transform that suffering into a blessing.

It's an important thing to be able to do. The Franciscan Fr. Richard Rohr reminds us that if suffering is not transformed it

14   Story sources: http://www.fdcc.org/in/canossiane/bakhita/bslave.htm and
     Catholic Digest

becomes suffering transmitted[15] — to those around us and to generations of people we will never meet. Anyone in Darfur, in Sr. Bakhita's Sudan, could probably tell us more than we'd want to know about the truth of that.

You might want to give Blessed Sister Josephine a call if you're suffering these days. I'm sure Jesus will be delighted to hear about you from a mutual friend like that.

I do need to tell you one last thing. The name *Bakhita* was not her real name. It had been given to her by the slave traders. It means 'Lucky.'

15 Richard Rohr, *From Wild Man to Wise Man*

Casey

The story's told of Casey, who had a problem with alcohol. Those who suffer from this disease know very well that it is a form of death, but Casey confused the illusion of life that alcohol gave him with the life that God had actually given him.

A distant family with alcoholic parents had left young Casey with little knowledge of how to cope with life. As he got older, Casey had built an alcohol-saturated world for himself in which the grandiose demands of his unconstrained infantile ego were consistently met to his satisfaction. Unfortunately, none of the real demands in his life were met.

Although he could function reasonably well, people could tell sooner or later that something wasn't right. Responsibilities were left unmet, relationships soured. He couldn't hold a job.

Fortunately for Casey, a close cousin recognized what was happening and arranged for Casey to get the help he needed. It wasn't easy for anyone. The help always requires people to hit bottom, and hit it hard. The lucky ones don't die.

As far as they're concerned though, they may as well have. The whole imaginary world Casey had built came crashing down around him, but he was able eventually to follow the twelve steps to sobriety, and remains clean to this day. He attributes his recovery to God.

When I asked him what it was like, turning his life around like that, he said "It's like coming back from the dead." There was so much catch-up and fence-mending to do.

He got thoughtful for a moment and added — "You know, it's like that story about Lazarus in the Bible. I was blessed to have a lot of people around me to help unwrap me from my shroud. They were there with me for the catch-up and they allowed me to do the fence-mending that needed to be done."

Mary's Two Stories

From time to time we are presented with opportunities to consider Mary's role in our salvation and how it connects to everyday life for you and me. What she did for us brought to mind a couple of stories I'd like to share with you.

The first one's about Brendan. Chances are you've never run into him. You'd remember if you had. Brendan's huge — about six-foot-six and 285 pounds — most of it muscle. As they say, you wouldn't want to meet him in a dark alley.

Unfortunately, someone did meet him in a dark alley up in Albany a few years back and didn't come out alive. That's why Brendan's in prison over in Attica, NY. Like his victim, Brendan won't be coming out of his dark alley alive, either: Brendan's in prison for life.

Brendan's story is familiar to those who do prison work. He came from a broken home. An abusive, mostly absent father and an alcoholic mother he could never count on to be there for him. That's what surrounded him as a child.

Beatings, ridicule, starvation for food and love — that's what Brendan remembered of his early life. Add to the mix an unhealthy dose of bad friends and dysfunctional relatives and you've got the recipe for disaster that defined Brendan's tender years and led him, eventually, to end up in prison.

In prison, like many others, Brendan found Jesus. He found out that Jesus had been there with him all along. He simply hadn't known where or how to look.

Brendan found someone else in prison, too. He found Mary. And in Mary, as he puts it, he found the mother he never had. "I found a mom I could count on," he says. "She led me through Jesus to a Father who was always there, and was never abusive. To someone who never ridiculed me. To someone who showed me how to give love and receive it. She's the best mom — the only real mom — I've ever had."

Most of us don't have a story quite like Brendan's. But we all do have a mom like the one he found in Mary. Scripture's clear about Mary's faithfulness to her mission both as an ordinary human being with a life not too different from yours and mine, and as God's specially chosen mother of his Son and of those who would follow him.

For Brendan, Mary was the mom he never had. For others she is the mom we've lost.

For even more people she is the mom we wish we had. For all of us she is the mom we really do have, always ready to take us gently by the hand and bring us to Jesus — to find him as he needs to be found. Let me tell you what I mean by that.

There's a fellow around my age, not too far from here, whose son, Tom, builds homes. Tom's wife teaches school so they frequently call on Tom's dad, Fred, to help watch their two little children, Alice and Tim.

One day he was doing that and the two little people told him they wanted to see the houses their dad was building. So Fred piled them into his car and took them over to the construction site.

As it turned out, they were drilling wells that day. Fred takes his Christianity pretty seriously and is always on the lookout for ways to help people, especially his children and grandchildren, snuggle up closer to the Lord. So when he saw the drilling equipment he smelled an opportunity.

Tim asked, "What are those, Grandpa?"

"Those are drilling rigs for wells, Tim" he said.

"There's water underground?" Tim asked, "How does it get there?"

"The water soaks into the ground from the rain and snow, kinda like the way God's grace soaks into all of us when we pray and especially when we receive communion."

"How do they know where to drill?" Alice wanted to know. "They can't see where the water is from up here."

"You're right, Alice. Some folks don't really know, but they just go ahead and drill anyway. The water's really down there, of course, but folks like that — well, sometimes they find the water, sometimes they don't. Other folks are wise enough to ask some-one to help them," Grandpa said.

"Who?" Tim asked.

"Someone who knows where the water is," Grandpa said, "someone who knows where to dig and how far down you have to go."

"That makes more sense," Alice said. "If you just dig and dig you'd never know if you were going to find water or not."

"Right," Grandpa said. "It's like when people look for Jesus; it's like that when we pray."

"What do you mean, Grandpa?" Tim asked.

"Well, you know when we pray the rosary together with Grandma?"

The children nodded.

"That's us asking our mom, Mary, to show us where to look for Jesus. She knows where we have to look and how far down we have to go to find the truth and goodness of God inside our-selves."

"She can see inside us?" Tim asked.

"Not really — but remember the story about Mary visiting her cousin Elizabeth? As she got near, John jumped inside Eliza-beth's tummy, didn't he?"

"I'll bet that hurt," Alice said.

"I don't know about that, "Grandpa said, "but the fact is that all Mary has to do is show up and stuff like that happens to peo-ple. They know they're around someone special."

"It's like us when we pray the rosary. When we're around her together, something special happens inside us, too. She takes us right to the spot where we have to dig with our thoughts and prayers to connect to the good and special truth, the grace, that's Jesus and his Father living within us."

"Then just like the water that will come up from the well your Dad's drilling over there, the grace of God will come up from the well Mary helps us dig inside ourselves. Just like we need water from the well for our bodies to live, we need the grace of God for our spirits to live."

Mary carries the responsibility and privilege of bearing Jesus to us with such winsome grace and humility. She knows where he is to be found, and she'll happily make the trip to you and me, just the way she did to her cousin, Elizabeth, so that you and I can have that special awakening within us, too.

Take a look at Mary again this Christmas, perhaps with a different set of eyes. Maybe you'll come to find as Brendan did, as I did one day long ago, and perhaps as many of you have also found out over time, that we all have a mother we perhaps never really knew we had – the best mom anyone could ever hope for.

The Second Coming

Many folks around my age have had the experience of looking all over the house for their glasses, only to be told by someone that we're already wearing them. If something like that hasn't ever happened to you, be patient: it will.

There's a story about a pastor who wanted to dramatize to his parishioners how we can miss seeing the Lord among us as easily as we can miss the glasses sitting on our nose, so he leaned on the rules a bit, hoping to shock his flock into an understanding of the inner meaning of stories about the second coming.

One Sunday he announced from the pulpit that he had received a letter from the archbishop that he had been told to read at all the masses that day. He warned the people that under pain of mortal sin they were not to disclose its contents to anyone.

Of course he hadn't really received any letter, but he knew he'd get their attention if he went at it this way. The alleged letter read like this — the names have been changed to protect the innocent:

Dear Father Smith,

We have been informed by the Congregation for the Propagation of the Faith in Rome that the second coming of Jesus is in progress. It seems that the location of the next appearance of our Lord is to be in your parish. Although we do not know the actual date and time, we are given to understand that it is to be very soon, and there is good reason to believe that he is actually among you at this very moment. There is no need to panic.

His Holiness, the Supreme Pontiff, and I trust that you and your parishioners will simply greet our Lord with the same joy and gratitude with which you customarily receive the Eucharist.

To avoid widespread disruption we require that you and your parishioners keep this information to yourselves and behave as you ordinarily would, simply with the additional knowledge that Jesus is most likely already among you.

Yours in Christ,
Archbishop James Beam

The pastor looked up and saw pretty much what he expected. Some folks were aghast at the thought that Jesus might be right there in the next pew. But most of the folks simply nodded and smiled back at the pastor, understanding just as I expect you do, exactly what he was really telling them.

Uh-Oh

Today marks the end of the church year, and the thought of it put me in mind of a cartoon that appeared in the New Yorker magazine many years ago that showed a man standing on the veranda of a beautiful tropical resort, looking at a gorgeous sunset. Across the sun were the words "THE END," and the caption read "Uh-Oh."

The church does want us to reflect on our lives and personal ends, but she'd like us to do that more with hope than with hysteria. As Christians, and like the repentant criminal at Jesus' side on Calvary, we all believe that it's through faith in Jesus that our hope for the future really lies, and we ought to be able to pursue this reflection with less anxiety than our friend in the cartoon.

The church invites us to do our reflection in the light of the meaning of the kingdom of God and acceptance of the kingship of Jesus. We should be mindful that although earthly realms are populated by people who were born there, got conquered or were intimidated into being subjects, the kingdom of God is populated only by volunteers.

If the realms are different, so are the rulers. It's clear that God's definition of a king is completely different than ours. Because our acceptance of Jesus is an act of love, our attraction to Jesus has to be based solely upon who he is and what he promises, not on displays of wealth and power. God's definition of our king is that he's the one who is totally for us. One who is completely giving of himself for those who love him.

No threats, no compulsion — only the open invitation to love, trust and hope. That's part of the reason why God came to us as a baby. What could be less threatening, or more loveable? That is part of the reason the king had to suffer and die — so that there could be nothing that would attract our love and admiration because of earthly accomplishments. Who would be attracted by the worldly merits of a man completely abandoned by his followers being executed between two criminals?

The good criminal listened to the taunts of the leaders and the soldiers. He heard his fellow criminal snarl with disgust at Jesus to save them all. But he realized that salvation to them merely meant to escape death and disgrace in the eyes of humans. Temporary relief at best. There'd be another crucifix down the road.

He sensed with clarity the reality of his situation. His sunset had THE END written all over it. And in a dramatic leap of faith and hope, he called upon Jesus with a humble and contrite heart simply to remember him — to take him beyond the horizon of the here-and-now where the other people's vision stopped.

Jesus' response to the good criminal's plea for friendship and mercy is that promise we all would love to hear someday — this day you shall be with me in paradise. Therein lies the key to the true meaning of the kingship of Jesus. Only a ruler of destinies could make such a promise, and only a ruler burning with love for us could do so for the most undeserving specimen of humanity — a criminal — while in the process of being murdered.

The good criminal addresses Jesus by name, like a friend. Curiously, it's the only time in any of the gospels that Jesus is addressed like that. The rest of the time he is "Lord," "Master," or some such thing. But at the intimate hour of death, Jesus would much prefer to be addressed as a personal friend. In fact, it's better if we do that all along, not just at the end.

A while back, a friend of mine told me a story about this friendly bond between Jesus and us. It seems he was attending a Bible study class at Saint Thomas Seminary in Bloomfield. There was a woman in the class with whom he'd struck up an acquaintance. As the class continued, he learned that her husband had been suffering from cancer.

With each class, the outlook for his recovery seemed less and less hopeful. It was a sad time to be sure — no one likes to see another suffer like that — but they had complete confidence in the Lord and trusted in a good outcome whatever it might turn out to be.

Her husband had always had a close relationship with Jesus. When he prayed, it was with the same trusting familiarity that we experience when we confide in really good friends or family.

One day, she visited him in the hospital. She could sense that the end was near, but he was perfectly lucid and wasn't feeling sorry for himself, though he was concerned for her. A nurse interrupted the conversation and gestured for her to come to the door to discuss medications and other sensitive issues. While she was talking with the nurse, she could hear her husband conversing out loud with someone, but she couldn't make out what he was saying. She didn't recall that there had been anyone else in the room.

When she finished talking to the nurse, she went back to her husband and asked him with whom he had been talking. "Jesus," he said. She was taken aback, but before she could get another question out he said: "He was right over there where you are now. He's coming to take me home next Tuesday. Oh, and you'll be fine." The next Tuesday he was gone, and as far as his wife is concerned these days, she's just fine.

Now, as the mileage estimate sticker says on new cars, your experience of the end may differ. But you should know that Jesus is quite alive and looking after his good friends. Come and receive him into your hearts — renew your friendship! And when the sunset comes for each of us, and it must, let Jesus, the king like no other king, call us by name out to the veranda and point to the sky, where the words will not be "THE END," but rather "THE BEGINNING" of something very, very good.

Open Heart Surgery

A few weeks ago at the hospital, I was called up to the room of a young man who was going to go in for open-heart surgery the next day. He wanted the sacrament of the sick and he wanted to pray. I called a priest, who said he'd come right in and administer the sacrament, and in the meantime we talked and prayed together.

It turns out that his heart had been compromised many years ago by a series of illnesses. His doctor had told him that the only way he would be able to live a normal life was to have a heart transplant. He didn't see that he had much choice, so he agreed. After waiting for several months, a heart was available for him.

"I'm scared," he told me. "They're going to replace my heart tomorrow."

I asked him to tell me about that.

"Maybe I'll die. Maybe there will be too much pain for me to bear, I just don't know. I've been so sick for so long, I don't even remember what feeling well is like," he said, "I can't even imagine it. Maybe I'm even a little afraid of that, too. It's hard, not knowing."

I nodded. Then he got reflective for a few moments, looked at me and said.

"You know, someone else had to die for me to be able to have a heart." He got quiet as he considered his own words. "Someone volunteered to give me his heart. I hope I can live a life worthy of that kind of generosity."

I knew from his chart that he was a Catholic, so I asked him if he saw any parallel between what he was about to undergo and anything God might've done in the past, or might be doing now, as we spoke.

"Are you saying you think my heart donor is like Jesus?" he asked. He thought about it quietly for a moment and then said "Maybe you're right. Like the death of the person whose heart I'll get tomorrow let just me live, Jesus gave his life so that everyone could live. Interesting. A different kind of living, but somehow the same kind of giving. I'm so very grateful. I wish I could thank him — I wish I could thank Jesus — in person."

I suggested to him that the resurrected Jesus was present to him in all the wonderful people who were taking care of him in the ICU, not to mention his donor.

"I wish there was some way I could see that plainly," he said. "Then maybe I could believe what you're saying."

Just then the priest arrived to administer the sacrament of the sick, along with a nurse to check his vitals.

"It doesn't get any plainer than that," I said with a smile, pointing to the priest and the nurse. "You can reach out and touch them."

A look of understanding began to dawn on his face. He looked at me and the priest and the nurse and smiled. "Jesus is all over the place, isn't he?"

"Yep," I agreed, "No doubt."

Tommy's Duty[16]

In 1805, as the Battle of Trafalgar got under way, Admiral Lord Nelson told his signal officer, Lt. John Pasco, to run up the message to his fleet, "England expects every man to do his duty." And so he did.

You can see those words for yourself if you travel to Trafalgar Square in London and take a look at the monument in the center of the square. As today's gospel reminds us, there's a time simply to do your duty; generally a time when everything hangs in the balance.

Little Tommy learned his lesson about duty a few years ago. One day he woke up and decided that he deserved compensation for all the chores he did around the house. So he wrote up a bill to give to his parents:

Taking out the garbage:	$1.65
Cleaning my room:	$2.00
Washing the dishes:	$2.35

Mom and Dad owe Tommy $6.00, payable upon receipt.

That evening, before he went to bed, Tommy taped the bill to his parents' bedroom door, confident that his parents would find it and understand their duty.

And understand they did. Tommy's parents are not unlike you: wise and gentle people who know right from wrong, with a good sense of humor but pretty direct too, when the need arises. So when Tommy awoke the next morning, he found an envelope on the nightstand next to his bed. Inside the envelope were six dollars and a note.

Tommy eagerly counted the six dollars again and again, imagining all the things he could buy. Mom and Dad were pretty cool, he thought. They really understood.

Then he read the note. It was a bill from Mom and Dad, and it read like this:

16 The billing motif is not original. Packaging and war story is original.

For feeding Tommy three meals a day, every day … Nothing
For taking care of Tommy when he was sick … Nothing
For teaching Tommy how to field a grounder … Nothing
For teaching Tommy about Jesus … Nothing

The list went on for a while. In each case, the amount Tommy owed Mom and Dad was 'Nothing.' The last items on the list were:

For doing our duty as Mom and Dad, Tommy owes us
Nothing

For the fabulous privilege of life and love, Tommy owes God
Everything

Cut to the quick, Tommy ran downstairs and found his mom and dad at the breakfast table. He tearfully gave them both a big hug, apologized for what he had done and handed them the six dollars.

His mom and dad are good, like you, so they just hugged him back and laughed with joy. Six dollars was pretty reasonable these days for a lesson in what duty means, they told him. Then they got a bit serious, the way parents do sometimes, and told Tommy that he could keep the money, but never let go of what he had learned about duty. He promised them he'd remember.

Tommy showed his parents what he'd learned about seventeen years later, when he came back from Iraq the way no parents should ever have to see their child come home.

At the funeral they were met by a young soldier, who gave them an envelope Tommy had asked him to give to his parents if something happened and he didn't make it back alive. As he handed it to them, he told them that Tommy had leapt without hesitation on the grenade that would've killed them both. He owed Tommy his life.

Mom and Dad opened the envelope slowly. Inside were six dollars and a note. The note said:

Dear Mom and Dad,

For taking care of me when I was little, Mom and Dad owe Tommy
…Nothing

For showing me what love means in everything you did, Mom and
Dad owe Tommy
… Nothing

For allowing me to love you too, Mom and Dad owe Tommy
…Nothing

For teaching me what Jesus did for all of us, Mom and Dad owe
Tommy
…Nothing

What Mom and Dad and Tommy owe Jesus
…Everything

You taught me about duty when I was little, and I never forgot.
You told me that Jesus gave everything he had for us, and that we
had to be ready to give everything too. I know now, and so do you,
what that might come to mean. Thank you for allowing me to be in
the circle of your love. You're the best parents anyone could ever
have had. I will pray for you, and I ask you to pray for me too. I
love you and will never forget you. Seems to me it's just my duty."

Love,
Tommy

In times like ours, when greed runs rampant and so many
people think only of themselves, when thugs kill their own citi-
zens to cling to power and the guilty work tirelessly to cover their
tracks, Tommy's story reminds us that we do well to remember
the law of love, and its requirement that you and I simply do our
duty.

Too Busy To Pray

I read something a while back that said "if you're too busy to pray, you're too busy to be a Christian." I happened to be pretty busy at the time, balancing a couple of different projects and trying to meet some tough deadlines.

So I didn't think kind thoughts about what seemed to me just then to be some crabby make-believe wisdom coming from some spiteful little troll who thought that all Christians should do things exactly the way he did them.

It was clear to me that this person had never had to drive three kids to four games that all started at the same time. This person had never had a job with conflicting priorities and alarming deadlines. This person had never had to take care of a sick child or ailing parents while managing a household and holding down a full-time job. This person knew nothing at all about what "busy" meant, and I tossed the book aside in disgust.

As it turned out, that particular week got enormously stressful for me, and I was afraid I'd be missing a deadline or two. There was simply no way to get all the work done. So I called to God in my distress and fully expected him to rescue me somehow. And he did, but not the way I thought he'd go about it.

I remember praying, "Look God, I've got way too much stuff on my plate. I'm out of hours and I can't handle it. Someone's going to be disappointed here if I can't get it all done. I need all the help I can get. Thanks in advance!"

The answer I got, as clearly as if you and I were chatting here after mass or something, was "No problem, Tim. Do this: spend an extra hour a day in prayer with me."

I was shocked. I prayed back, "Look...God...I just got finished telling you how busy I was and you're telling me to spend an extra hour a day in prayer? Let me use small words: I'm out of hours. I don't have any more to give you."

The answer came back: "How long have we been together, Tim?"

"As long as I can remember," I said.

"Have I ever disappointed you?" God asked.

"Only the time when I was ten and asked for wings, but I'm glad now that you didn't give them to me," I replied. "But this is different."

"I know," God said. "It needs to be different, Tim. Spend the hour, would you?"

I said I would and went off shaking my head, wondering about the ways of your Creator and mine.

So off I went to a quiet place and spent an extra hour in prayer the next day. I decided to use an old formula a nun had taught a bunch of us many years ago: rest, read, reflect, and relish.

Rest for twenty minutes. Simply do nothing. Go to that quiet place to which Jesus was taking the disciples in the gospel. Spend twenty minutes just idly paying attention to your breathing, gently deferring thoughts that creep up, without criticism and without trying to crush them. No phone, no computer, no radio, TV, iPod or anything like that. Just quiet time, taking God up on His invitation to be still and know that He is God.

After that, yawn, stretch, and read a passage from the Bible. Reflect for a while on what it might mean, without manufacturing an answer. Not having a clue what it means is a perfectly acceptable circumstance. Just spend the time — that's what's important.

Then spend a few happy moments in the palm of God's hand. Relish the fact that you're enjoying the privilege of spending time with the God who created and loves you; who's always glad to spend time with you. Trust that whatever needed to be done for you just then, as only God can know, God has done. Then go pick up your shovel and head back to the mine.

When I did that, I noticed an interesting phenomenon. I did what I thought was a full day's work, without ever looking at my watch. When I did finally look at it, I was astonished to see that it wasn't even eleven AM yet.

My extra hour of prayer had left me calm, focused, peaceful, and full of energy.

God had taken my hour and multiplied it into what it needed to be for all the work on my plate to get done. I could tell that if things kept up like this, I wouldn't miss any deadlines at all; I'd finish with plenty of time to spare. I was awed, and for what I'm certain is not the last time in my life, deeply humbled and grateful to God.

So we talked about it a while later. I told God I was sorry for being a wise-guy and he told me not to worry, he liked to do that himself sometimes. Then I asked what work I should do next, in his opinion. The answer was again straight out of today's gospel, and God used small words so that I'd understand.

"Do the work that will help others first," God said. "Then do your own stuff."

It's what Jesus did when he got out of the boat and was moved with compassion for his people. He did the work that his people so desperately needed him to do. The Greek expression that describes how Jesus felt just then literally means "he was moved to the core of his being," which is the place within us where God and humans mix; the place we access in prayer.

I could see then that the extra hour in prayer I'd been asked to spend was not just a mind-calming energy booster. It was the way I could get my priorities straight, come to see what work really had to be done, and get service to others back where it belonged, in front of service to self. In prayer I could receive from God all the energy to do everything God needed me to do that day, in the order it needed to be done, calmly, efficiently and peacefully.

I thought of that expression I'd read earlier, "If you're too busy to pray, you're too busy to be a Christian." I still didn't like it all that much. We're all baptized and we're Christians, for keeps.

My own experience made me think that since God so enjoys being together with us, maybe he would say something kinder and gentler to us, like this: "I know you think you're too busy to pray and maybe you really are. But come away to a quiet place and just spend an extra hour a day with me anyway. You may be astonished at what happens next!"

Index

This is where the stories showed up in the homilies. If it's useful at all, it's perhaps just that you might see connections similar to those I saw at the time. I hope that if you use the stories, you make them your own. Mix and match to your heart's content, and by all means add your own experiences to them. They're nothing more than seeds that happen to have fallen on your infinitely fertile soil.

Dogs	20 Ordinary A	Isa 56:1, 6-7; Rom 11:13-15, 29-32; Matt 15:21-28
The Best Of Neighbors	24 Ordinary B	Isa 50:5-9a; Jam 2:14-18; Mark 8:27-35
Divorce	27 Ordinary B	Gen 2:18-24; Heb 2:9-11; Mark 10:2-16
Computer Wisdom	28 Ordinary B	Wis 7:7-11; Heb 4:12-13; Mark 10:17-30
Learning From The Pros	All Saints Day	Rev 7:2-4, 9-14; John 3:1-3; Matt 5:1-12a
Hospice	33 Ordinary B	Dan 12:1-3; Heb 10:11-14, 18; Mark 13:24-32
Get Out Of Jail Free	2 Advent C	Bar 5:1-9; Phil 1:4-6, 8-11; Luke 3:1-6
Chapel Miracle	28 Ordinary C	Kgs 5:14-17; 2Tim 2:8-13; Luke 17:11-19
Dave And The Football	3 Advent C	Zeph 3:14-18a; Phil 4:4-7; Luke 3:10-18
Gifts Of The Magi	Epiphany A	Isa 60:1-6; Eph 3:2-3a, 5-6; Matt 2:1-12
Do It Your Way	Passion Sunday B	Isa 50:4-7; Phil 2:6-11; Mark 14:1-15:47
Halloween	24 Ordinary B	Isa 50:5-9a; Jam 2:14-18; Mark 8:27-35
Who Are You?	3 Advent B	Isa 61:1-2a, 10-11; 1Thess 5:16-24; John 1:6-8, 19-28
Gina And The Leaves	33 Ordinary B	Dan 12:1-3; Heb 10:11-14, 18; Mark 13:24-32
Investments	1 Advent A	Isa 2:1-5; Rom 13:11-14; Matt 24:37-44
Patty And The Blind	4 Lent A	1 Sam 16:1b, 6-7, 10-13a; Eph 5:8-14; John 9:1-41
It's All Unconditional	13 Ordinary A	2 Kgs 4:8-11, 14-16a; Rom 6:3-4, 8-11; Matt 10:37-42
Perfect Little Annie	7 Ordinary A	Lv 19:1-2, 17-18; 1Cor 3:16-23; Matt 5: 38-48
The $20 Web	18 Ordinary C	Eccl 1:2, 2:21-23; Col 3:1-5, 9-11; Luke 12:13-21
God's Song	17 Ordinary C	Gen 18:20-32; Col 2:12-14; Luke 11:1-13
Soon And Never	13 Ordinary C	1 Kgs 19:16b, 19-21; Gal 5:1, 13-18; Luke 9:51-62
Trinity	Trinity Sunday C	Prv 8:22-31; Rom 5:1-5; John 16:12-15
Flashpoint	Pentecost C	Acts 2:1-11; 1Cor 12:3b-7, 12-13; John 20:19-23
Lucky	6 Ordinary C	Jer 17:5-8; 1 Cor 15:12, 16-20; Luke 6:17, 20-26
Casey	5 Lent A	Ezek 37:12-14; Rom 8:8-11; John 11:1-45
Mary's Two Stories	4 Advent C	Mic 5:1-4a; Heb 10:5-10; Luke 1:39-45
The Second Coming	1 Advent C	Jer 33:14-16; 1 Thess 3:12—4:2; Luke 21:25-28, 34-36
Uh-Oh	Christ the King C	Sam 5:1-3; Col 1:12-20; Luke 23:35-43
Open Heart Surgery	Easter 2 A	Acts 2:42-47; 1 Pet 1:3-9; John 20:19-31
Tommy's Duty	27 Ordinary C	Habb 1:2-3; 2:2-4; 2 Tim 1:6-8, 13-14; Luke 17:5-10
Too Busy To Pray	5 Ordinary B	Job 7:1-4, 6-7; 1Cor 9:16-19, 22-23; Mark 1:29-39

By Lectionary Reference

Story	Sunday	Readings
Investments	1 Advent A	Isa 2:1-5; Rom 13:11-14; Matt 24:37-44
Rocky	1 Advent B	Isa 63:16b-17, 19b; 64:2-7; 1 Cor 1:3-9; Mark 13:33-37
The Second Coming	1 Advent C	Jer 33:14-16; 1 Thess 3:12—4:2; Luke 21:25-28, 34-36
Get Out Of Jail Free	2 Advent C	Bar 5:1-9; Phil 1:4-6, 8-11; Luke 3:1-6
Who Are You?	3 Advent B	Isa 61:1-2a, 10-11; 1Thess 5:16-24; John 1:6-8, 19-28
Dave And The Football	3 Advent C	Zeph 3:14-18a; Phil 4:4-7; Luke 3:10-18
Mary's Two Stories	4 Advent C	Mic 5:1-4a; Heb 10:5-10; Luke 1:39-45
Tommy And John	Holy Family B	Sir 3:2-7, 12-14; Col 3:12-21; Luke 2:22-40
Gifts Of The Magi	Epiphany A	Isa 60:1-6; Eph 3:2-3a, 5-6; Matt 2:1-12
Patty and the Blind	4 Lent A	1 Sam 16:1b, 6-7, 10-13a; Eph 5:8-14; John 9:1-41

Tim At IBM	4 Lent Sunday B	2 Chr 36:14-16, 19-23; Eph 2:4-10; John 3:14-21
Casey	5 Lent A	Ezek 37:12-14; Rom 8:8-11; John 11:1-45
Hospital Visit	Passion Sunday B	Isa 50:4-7; Phil 2:6-11; Mark 14:1-15:47
Do It Your Way	Passion Sunday B	Isa 50:4-7; Phil 2:6-11; Mark 14:1-15:47
Tomás	Holy Thursday	Exod 12:1-8, 11-14; 1 Cor 11:23-26; John 13:1-15
Good Friday	Good Friday B	Isa 52:13—53:12; Heb 4:14-16; 5:7-9; John 18:1—19:42
Open Heart Surgery	Easter 2 A	Acts 2:42-47; 1 Pet 1:3-9; John 20:19-31
Two Stories	Divine Mercy Sunday	Acts 4:32-35; 1Jn 5:1-5; John 20:19-31
ESPN	Divine Mercy Sunday	Acts 5:12-16; Rev 1:9-11a. 12-13, 17-19; John 20:19-31
The Shield	4 Easter C	Acts 13:14, 43-52; Rev 7:9, 14b-17; John 10:27-30
The Check	6 Easter A	Acts 8:5-8, 14-17; 1Pet 3:15-18; John 14:15-21
Murphy The Grump	Pentecost A	Gen 11:1-9; Rom 8:22-27; John 7:37-39
The Maltese Falcon	Pentecost C	Acts 2:1-11; Rom 8:8-17; John 14:15-16, 23b-26
Flashpoint	Pentecost C	Acts 2:1-11; 1Cor 12:3b-7, 12-13; John 20:19-23
Samuel, Bill And Alice	2 Ordinary Sunday B	Sam 3:3b-10, 19; 1 Cor 6:13c-15a, 17-20; John 1:35-42
Too Busy To Pray	5 Ordinary B	Job 7:1-4, 6-7; 1Cor 9:16-19, 22-23; Mark 1:29-39
Katie	5 Ordinary C	Isa 6:1-2a, 3-8; 1Cor 15:1-11; Luke 5:1-11
Lucky	6 Ordinary C	Jer 17:5-8; 1 Cor 15:12, 16-20; Luke 6:17, 20-26
Perfect Little Annie	7 Ordinary A	Lv 19:1-2, 17-18; 1Cor 3:16-23; Matt 5: 38-48
Monsters Under The Bed	10 Ordinary A	Hos 6:3-6; Rom 4:18-25; Matt 9:9-13
Tommy And His Dad	12 Ordinary A	Exod 19:2-6a; Rom 5:6-11; Matt 9:36—10:8
It's All Unconditional	13 Ordinary A	2 Kgs 4:8-11, 14-16a; Rom 6:3-4, 8-11; Matt 10:37-42
Soon And Never	13 Ordinary C	1 Kgs 19:16b, 19-21; Gal 5:1, 13-18; Luke 9:51-62
Flying to Hawaii	14 Ordinary A	Zech 9:9-10; Rom 8:9, 11-13; Matt 11:25-30
Mr. Dobson	16 Ordinary A	Wis 12:13, 16-19; Rom 8:26-27; Matt 13:24-43
God's Song	17 Ordinary C	Gen 18:20-32; Col 2:12-14; Luke 11:1-13
Sandwiches	18 Ordinary A	Isa 55:1-3; Rom 8:35, 37-39; Matt 14:13-21
Loving The Right Way	18 Ordinary A	Isa 55:1-3; Rom 8:35, 37-39; Matt 14:13-21
The $20 Web	18 Ordinary C	Eccl 1:2, 2:21-23; Col 3:1-5, 9-11; Luke 12:13-21
Dogs	20 Ordinary A	Isa 56:1, 6-7; Rom 11:13-15, 29-32; Matt 15:21-28
Tim And Terri	21 Ordinary C	Isa 66:18-21; Heb 12:5-7, 11-13; Luke 13:22-30
Hatred	23 Ordinary C	Wis 9:13-18b; Phlm 9-10, 12-17; Luke 14:25-33
The Best Of Neighbors	24 Ordinary B	Isa 50:5-9a; Jam 2:14-18; Mark 8:27-35
Halloween	24 Ordinary B	Isa 50:5-9a; Jam 2:14-18; Mark 8:27-35
Vinnie And The AC	26 Ordinary A	Ezek 18:25-28; Phil 2:1-11; Matt 21:28-32
Divorce	27 Ordinary B	Gen 2:18-24; Heb 2:9-11; Mark 10:2-16
The Trophy	27 Ordinary C	Habb 1:2-3; 2:2-4; 2 Tim 1:6-8, 13-14; Luke 17:5-10
Tommy's Duty	27 Ordinary C	Habb 1:2-3; 2:2-4; 2 Tim 1:6-8, 13-14; Luke 17:5-10
Computer Wisdom	28 Ordinary B	Wis 7:7-11; Heb 4:12-13; Mark 10:17-30
Chapel Miracle	28 Ordinary C	Kgs 5:14-17; 2Tim 2:8-13; Luke 17:11-19
Mickey The Impressive	30 Ordinary C	Sir 35:12-14, 16-18; 2 Tim 4:6-8, 16-18; Luke 18:9-14
Brother Dave	32 Ordinary C	2 Macc 7:1-2, 9-14; 2 Thess 2:16—3:5; Luke 20:27-38
Hospice	33 Ordinary B	Dan 12:1-3; Heb 10:11-14, 18; Mark 13:24-32

Gina And The Leaves	33 Ordinary B	Dan 12:1-3; Heb 10:11-14, 18; Mark 13:24-32
Uh-Oh	Christ the King C	Sam 5:1-3; Col 1:12-20; Luke 23:35-43
Trinity	Trinity Sunday C	Prv 8:22-31; Rom 5:1-5; John 16:12-15
Alice And The Bean	Corpus Christi C	Gen 14:18-20; 1 Cor 11:23-26; Luke 9:11b-17
Emily	Exalt. of the Cross	Num 21:4b-9; Phil 2:6-11; John 3:13-17
Learning From The Pros	All Saints Day	Rev 7:2-4, 9-14; John 3:1-3; Matt 5:1-12a